THE DOG
WHO CAME TO
CHRISTMAS

Books by Callie Smith Grant

The Cat on My Lap

The Dog at My Feet

The Cat in the Window

The Dog Next Door

The Horse of My Heart

Second-Chance Dogs

The Horse of My Dreams

Second-Chance Cats

THE DOG WHO CAME TO CHRISTMAS

And Other True Stories of the Gifts Dogs Bring Us

CALLIE SMITH GRANT, Ed.

Revell

a division of Baker Publishing Group
Grand Rapids, Michigan

© 2021 by Baker Publishing Group

Published by Revell
a division of Baker Publishing Group
PO Box 6287, Grand Rapids, MI 49516-6287
www.revellbooks.com

Printed in the United States of America

Library of Congress Cataloging-in-Publication Data
Names: Grant, Callie Smith, editor.
Title: The dog who came to Christmas : and other true stories of the gifts dogs bring us / Callie Smith Grant, Ed.
Description: Grand Rapids, Michigan : Revell, a division of Baker Publishing Group, [2021] | Includes bibliographical references.
Identifiers: LCCN 2021004364 | ISBN 9780800737924 (paperback) | ISBN 9780800741259 (casebound) | ISBN 9781493431861 (ebook)
Subjects: LCSH: Dogs--Anecdotes. | Christmas. | Human-animal relationships.
Classification: LCC SF426.2 .D6465 2021 | DDC 636.7--dc23
LC record available at https://lccn.loc.gov/2021004364

Baker Publishing Group publications use paper produced from sustainable forestry practices and post-consumer waste whenever possible.

21 22 23 24 25 26 27   7 6 5 4 3 2 1

To the memory
of my beloved friend Richard,
who loved Christmas more
than any other adult I know.

CONTENTS

Contents

Contents

INTRODUCTION

Christmas and dogs.

I love both, so what a pleasure for me to collect stories about that wonderful combination.

As I write this, there's a whole lot of stress going on in our world. With so many troubles afoot, I will admit I tend to get extra anxious. To cope, I'm learning new skills to distract myself so that I'm not constantly mired in disturbing news.

One of the new tools (new to me anyway) I use to distract myself is my local newspaper's online comics page. I check the funnies every morning. This may not be the deepest way to deal with things, but I find starting my day with the smile this act provides is helpful and most likely healthy.

I begin with *The Family Circus*, where recently little Billy said, "The softest warmest pillow in the whole world are dogs."[1]

Isn't that the truth? What a gift dogs are.

In the same week, I happened upon a new research report that concluded children between the ages of two and five are less likely to have social-interaction issues if they are raised with a dog. How less likely? A whopping 40 percent.[2]

Now *there's* a reason to put a puppy under the Christmas tree!

Of course, we don't need to be children to appreciate dogs (and let's remember that we should always be cautious with surprise pets for presents). In these pages you'll meet people of all ages who had the privilege of interacting in beautiful, memorable ways with a dog or puppy, new or known, at Christmastime.

You'll meet some young families with not much money, but they receive a gift—a lively, furry new family member who offers unconditional love to all. You'll meet one mom who hides a surprise Christmas puppy in a stable—reminding her afresh of the earthiness of the place of the Christ child's birth. One writer's extreme shyness about meeting her potential new in-laws at Christmas is eased by the actions of an extraordinary dog who pulls the whole new family together.

Some dogs are true friends to their humans for the dog's entire life. Some dogs are there only for a season—maybe only for the Christmas season. They all offer their unique gifts of love and support, of companionship, even of life to their loved ones. Or sometimes to strangers. Or even more remarkably, sometimes to other animals.

And yes, a couple of stories really do feature boxes with dogs in them under the tree on Christmas morning. But we also learn there's more than one way to get a dog for Christmas. You'll see!

A gentle warning: There is occasional heartbreak scattered throughout these pages. But let me assure you—no hearts were broken permanently in the writing of this book. Why? Because of dogs. They can be the great healers of hearts.

Christmas thoughts seemed to remind some of the contributors of beloved dogs loved and lost. But so many of them tell how they went on to love another wonderful dog. As contributor Andi Lehman's father tells her, "The greatest tribute you can pay an animal you loved and lost is to love another." Some stories feature new dogs redeeming loss.

Christmas and dogs. What a gift. As contributor Lisa Begin-Kruysman says in her story, "The gift of dog is that they remind us there is no time like the present and no present like time."

I trust you'll enjoy these stories as much as I have enjoyed them. Reading them has been another unexpected tool—a gift, really—to get me through the stress of the times. Thank you for that, dear contributors.

Have a blessed Christmas, all.

Callie Smith Grant

1

Bailey's House

Melody Carlson

Bailey the dog had been our "baby" for more than six years when a granddaughter came into our lives. And although this oversized lab was the sweetest dog imaginable, I think his nose was just slightly out of joint for being displaced by a real baby. He didn't know what to make of this noisy little bundle who seemed to be getting all the attention. Especially when Christmastime arrived.

Our Bailey was solidly built with a shiny chocolate-colored coat and a happy smile. Adored by family and friends for his gentle disposition, he was the kind of dog who liked everyone. Bailey was useless as a watchdog, and we always joked that if a burglar intruded, our dog would just wag his tail and lead him to the silver.

Like any beloved child, Bailey had his own Christmas stocking. Nothing fancy but always filled with some special treats for Christmas—usually something to chew on and a plush doggy toy. Although most of the doggy toys seemed to go missing . . . eventually.

But this particular year, we had our new grandbaby in the house. Not only was Baby Anika stealing some of the attention away from Bailey, but Bailey had probably been spending a bit more time in the laundry room than usual too. Not that he was neglected exactly, but he just wasn't the center of attention like he was used to being.

My mother had knitted Anika a beautiful Christmas stocking that I'd hung on the mantel with the other hand-knit stockings. But a couple days before Christmas, that new stocking went missing. The rest were still in place—but Anika's was mysteriously gone. That's when I remembered how I'd spotted one of Anika's favorite baby toys out in Bailey's dog run a few days earlier. The plush yellow duckling (it sang "Singin' in the Rain") had been lying beak-down in the snow. I rescued the kidnapped duck to find it was in good shape and still able to sing.

Curious about the missing stocking, I looked out the kitchen window, and there on the freshly fallen snow was the red-and-green sock. Relieved to find it was in perfect condition, I gave Bailey a good-natured scolding, then returned it to its hook with the others. That's when I noticed Bailey's stocking hadn't even been hung yet. Was he trying to give me a hint? So before long, Bailey's Christmas stocking was hanging too, and we all had a good laugh over it.

Christmas came and went. The following weekend, I joined my mother and sister for a little getaway, and that evening my sister asked if I'd liked my Christmas present from her. Caught off guard, I tried to remember her gift—but came up blank. She described the packaging (she's known for beautiful wrapping), and she informed me that it contained a very special handmade bracelet. "And there was something in there for Bailey too," she said with concern.

Suddenly I remembered how Bailey had snitched Anika's duck and Christmas stocking, and I wondered if he'd taken anything else. It seemed out of character since he'd never been that kind of dog before. But having a baby around had been an adjustment for him. I called home and explained the mystery to my husband. He promised to do some investigating and called me back a few minutes later.

Now I must pause to explain that Bailey's kennel wasn't just an ordinary kennel. It started with a doggy-door that led from the laundry room to a pretty nice doghouse (with two rooms). And that led out into a large, fenced dog run where he could freely come and go. Pretty posh for a dog.

"I found the wrapping paper and ribbon and box outside," my husband told me. "So I could tell Bailey was responsible." But he explained that the items that were supposed to be inside the box were missing. "I crawled into Bailey's doghouse with my flashlight. I found the bracelet and a leather dog collar with beadwork that says 'Good Dog.'"

Of course, we had a good laugh over that one. The "Good Dog" who'd stolen a present from beneath the Christmas tree. My husband reassured me that both items were in excellent condition. "He didn't chew them or anything. But what surprised me even more was that he'd decorated his doghouse."

"Decorated his doghouse?" I wondered if I'd heard him right.

"Yeah. You know the boxes of Christmas decorations that you'd left in the laundry room?"

"The ones that just had leftover decorations?" I asked.

"It looks like Bailey helped himself to some of those decorations. And he's put them in his doghouse."

"You're kidding!"

He laughed. "No, I'm serious. Bailey *decorated* his doghouse."

It took a few seconds for this to even register. "So Bailey found his Christmas present under the tree, opened it, then took it into his doghouse that he'd already decorated?"

"And that's not all," my husband said.

"There's more?"

"Yeah. Bailey's got a collection too."

"A collection?"

Now my husband laughingly described how Bailey had all his plush doggy toys—the toys that he'd gotten for previous Christmases and the stuffed toys that had gone missing—all lined up in a neat little row.

"They're all clean and in great condition," he said with wonder. "Almost as if Bailey and the toys were having a Christmas party together."

After that, we always made sure Bailey had a new toy for Christmas each year. When Bailey died about five years later, my husband went out to clean Bailey's doghouse—but he couldn't do it. Because there, lined neatly along one wall inside the doghouse, sat all of Bailey's stuffed toys: a duck, a moose, a bear, and a couple of others—almost like gifts beneath a Christmas tree.

We decided to leave the doggy toys alone. Maybe it was a memorial of sorts. We were certain we'd never get another dog—the heartbreak was too much. But then a two-year-old yellow lab named Audrey entered our lives. When she found Bailey's lineup of toys, she selected only one—the duck—to bring into the house. Then shortly before Christmas, she took the duck back out to the doghouse. And when I peeked out there, just like Bailey, she kept her toys all together like presents piled under the Christmas tree.

It just makes you wonder . . .

2

Birds of a Different Feather

Kathrine Diedre Smith

When I was a young woman, I became engaged to a special man. I'm not quite sure what he ever saw in me, but we were in love. He wanted to spend the Christmas immediately following our engagement with his extended family, whom I had never met. To say that I was nervous would be quite an understatement.

I was painfully shy and felt terribly awkward. My fiancé's family wanted to know everything about me, where I came from, how Brian and I were meant for each other, and what we all had in common. I didn't know how to answer them. When I thought about it, I really wasn't certain what I had in common with the family. They were seriously into aviation. Brian and his father flew planes and even owned several. I was terrified of flying, especially in small planes. His sister was a debutante; I was a simple country girl and a tomboy. His mom was the quintessential homemaker and cook, while I could barely heat a can of soup. The thought of spending Christmas in a part of Texas where the winters can be bone-chillingly cold, knowing no one else, where I didn't seem to have anything in common with these people other than their son . . . well, I was kind of terrified.

I had a dog at the time, a big, beautiful black Labrador retriever I had saved when he was about six months old. I had found him alone in a park early one Sunday morning, skinny, trembling, and extremely fearful. He cowered away with his head to his chest and his tail tightly between his legs every time I spoke to him. When I tried to get close to him, he ran away. I spent the better part of the day trying to encourage him to come out.

That evening, I borrowed someone's friendly dog and went back to the park where I'd found the homeless dog. He was still there, still terribly fearful. It seemed obvious that he had been beaten. Eventually, with the help of the friendly dog, I was able to get the lab to approach me. I brought food, and the poor dog practically inhaled it, he was so hungry. When I turned to leave, he started following me. I didn't know if he had been dumped, but it was evident that he hadn't received any love or care.

He followed me for about a mile to my studio apartment. Once home, I invited him inside. He was such a scrawny, scrappy boy, at that awkward late-adolescent stage, no longer an adorable puppy. Living in a college community, I had discovered it was not unusual for pets, even purebreds, to be abandoned toward the end of the semester. Still, I gave the benefit of the doubt and posted lost-and-found flyers and ran an ad in our local newspaper in case he belonged to someone. No one ever claimed him. So he became my family.

He was the first dog I had ever rescued or owned. After having him for a number of weeks, I had tried calling him many names, but he just ignored them. One day, out of frustration from trying out so many other "cool" names, I blurted out, "Well, you're just a *maximum dog*, aren't you?" With that, he turned around and sat squarely at my feet. So that's how Max got his name.

My fiancé, Brian, insisted that it would be okay to take Max to his parents' house, even though they didn't have a dog and didn't have any experience with a large dog. Max had grown up and filled out by then. No longer awkward or fearful, he was a loyal, confident, and trusted companion. I didn't want to impose, but secretly I thought it would be nice to have at least one more familiar face nearby so I wouldn't have to lean on my fiancé exclusively for support.

We loaded up the car and drove five and a half hours to Brian's family's home. Everyone was there. His parents, siblings, even his grandparents from Arizona! They were all supersocial, chatty, and full of questions. I didn't know what I had gotten myself into. Thankfully, we had a practical reason to step away and go outside periodically to take breaks—one of the benefits of having a large dog. They need fresh air and the opportunity to stretch their legs, and so do I.

Early Christmas morning, Brian's brother and sister wanted to join us on our early morning walk with Max. It was nice to get away from the house and explore the neighborhood. I had taught Max to walk off lead, and he was very good at maintaining a close natural heel.

About thirty minutes into our walk, Max trotted away from me, which wasn't unusual when he needed to do his "business." But this time, he went inside a stranger's open garage. That was highly unusual for Max. I called out to him, but he didn't come back right away. I called to him again, and this time he came, but with something completely filling his mouth. It was a mockingbird, and it was stuck in a glue trap.

As soon as Brian and his siblings saw two tiny feet and the sticky trap, Brian said, "Well, that's one dead bird." I thought, *Not so fast*. Max was holding that bird ever so gently and had found a way to carry it to me, trap and all, in his ginormous mouth. He brought this helpless, tiny creature who was completely stuck and quietly handed me his rescue while gazing directly into my eyes, as if to say, *You fix it, Mom*.

Though he was a little moist from being in the mouth of a Labrador, the mockingbird wasn't bleeding and didn't have any breaks, punctures, or damage to his body. The problem was that the bird's tiny legs were completely stuck in the glue trap, and I needed to figure out a way to safely remove them.

We headed back to Brian's parents' house, now full of commotion over the bird Max had rescued. Thankfully, his parents led me to an enclosed area where I could work on the stuck bird. Suddenly everyone was on board, trying to figure out a way to help me get the glue off the fragile legs and feet without harming the bird. We used a mild dish soap and hand creams but with only partial success. Then I thought about using vinegar. Someone found a convenience store that was open on Christmas day and bought a small container of vinegar. I used soft cloths moistened in vinegar and placed that over the gooey, sticky adhesive.

Finally, it started to loosen. I went through so many soft cloths and dabs of vinegar in this intricate and painstaking process. Max lay at my feet the entire time, gently nudging and reassuring me throughout. Eventually, I was able to get all the glue off the mockingbird's legs, as well as each individual toe and teeny nail. After all the icky glue was removed, I rinsed his legs off with warm water and patted them dry.

By this time, no one could believe the bird had lived through this entire ordeal, and the awkwardness with everyone began to melt away, just like the glue from the sticky trap. Once all the glue had been successfully removed, the bird suddenly became energized and feisty, and the entire family wanted to be part of his release.

So on that most memorable Christmas day, we went out together, led by a big beautiful black dog, and released the bird he'd rescued. And the bird flew! High up and far away, and we all waved as that mockingbird soared. Thanks to a rescue dog named Max, we became a family that year and celebrated a Christmas miracle together.

3

Bulldog Christmas

DeVonna R. Allison

A light snow lay around our little home in the woods on the week before Christmas. It was a Friday evening, and approaching headlights told us someone was winding their way up our driveway. Wrapped against the cold, I stepped out onto the porch, where the smell of woodsmoke hung in the air. My husband Earl's boots squeaked in the snow as he joined me on the porch.

We recognized our daughter's car. The car door opened, and before we could greet one another, the unmistakable form of a bulldog bounded out into the snow. The dog wriggled and danced in greeting as we stared, openmouthed.

Our daughter explained, breathless. "I found her wandering in a parking lot in town, trying to climb into people's cars. There's something wrong with her, but she's so sweet . . ."

The frown on Earl's face said just how unwelcome our canine visitor was. Earl wasn't looking for a dog. Our ten-year-old

American pit bull terrier, Ebony Rose, had died in the spring of that year. Nine months later, the loss was still fresh for my husband. Ebony had been his faithful shadow, and although our grown children and I had urged Earl to adopt another dog, my husband was firm.

"We don't need another dog, especially a sick one," he now said.

"Can't you just take her in for the night?" our daughter pled. "I don't want her going to the pound, especially at Christmas."

Whether it was mention of our local animal control or the season, I'm not sure, but Earl said, "Well, just for the one night. And not in the house."

The bulldog trotted behind us toward the garage. There, in the light, we could see the full extent of her sorry condition. Her short white coat was falling away in patches. Her skin was crusted, inflamed, and oozing. Her eyes ran, and she held her head in such a funny way I wondered if she could hear us clearly. Moreover, the dog was crawling with fleas.

Her miserable condition was in stark contrast to her happy attitude. She seemed overjoyed to be with us. Earl made up a soft bed for the dog, and we shut her in for the night. Checking in on her later, Earl said he found her curled up on her makeshift bedding, emitting loud snores.

The next morning Earl was up early.

"I'll bet that dog has made a mess of my garage," he grumbled, pulling on his boots and coat.

I wrapped my fingers around my cup of hot coffee and watched through the kitchen window. The dog greeted Earl at the door of the garage, her face spread in a wide bully grin. As it turned out, she'd had no accidents in the garage and even took her business to the far corner of the yard. My husband was impressed.

After sniffing around in her new environment, the dog trotted up to Earl and went down on her front legs, an obvious attempt to play. It didn't take much convincing on her part. Soon she and Earl were running and playing in the snow together.

My husband came in, his cheeks bright red from the cold and exertion, and asked, "How soon can you be ready to go to town?"

"To town?" I was still in my robe.

"We've got to get that dog to the vet," Earl said, as if it were the most natural thing in the world.

I drove the eight miles to town with my husband beside me cradling the bulldog's raw, scaly head. He spoke to her soothingly while Christmas carols played over the radio.

"So what should we call her?" I asked.

"We're not naming her because we're not keeping her," Earl insisted.

A smile crept into the corners of my mouth unbidden, and I said no more.

The waiting room of our vet's office was decorated with tinseled garlands, twinkle lights, and greeting cards. We were the only ones in the room and didn't have to wait long.

Under the bright lights of the exam room, the doctor confirmed the dog appeared to be an English bulldog probably crossed with another bully breed. He guessed her age to be about one and a half years. He scrutinized the dog's ears and eyes, took her temperature, and checked her teeth.

The vet took a skin scraping and disappeared into his lab to look at the sample under a microscope. The news was not great. The dog was covered in demodectic mange. It would require lengthy and expensive treatments to cure her. She also had a severe double ear infection in addition to the flea infestation. In short, she was a mess. My hopes for keeping the dog plummeted with the news of her condition.

Our veterinarian laid out clearly what treatments she would require and then asked, "What do you call her?"

I opened my mouth to explain we weren't keeping the dog, but Earl spoke first. "Her name is Molly," he said, and we smiled at each other.

On the way home, we stopped at the local farm store where Earl bought bowls, food, and toys for Molly, plus a thick, cushiony bed.

Over the next few months Molly received chemical dips to treat the mange, along with antibiotics, steroids, and flea treatments. She made a complete recovery, and her coat filled in clean and white with a brindle spot above one eye. With her distinctive bulldog grin, she is quite a sight! She is Earl's constant companion, but best of all, she's a healthy, happy dog. And of course she lives in the house now.

One year after we gave Molly a home, Earl took her to have her picture taken with Santa Claus. We display the picture on our mantel every year at Christmastime. It never fails to put a smile on our faces because it reminds us of our first bulldog Christmas.

4

Fafnir's Christmas Gift

Amy Shojai

Newlyweds always face challenges learning what to expect from each other. My husband, Mahmoud, came from a country, culture, and family very different from the close-knit, pet-loving household I'd experienced. But we had faith our love was enough to build a life together.

Five months into our marriage, our world blew up. We struggled to understand the taking of hostages half a world away, and we worried about Mahmoud's relatives caught in the insanity of that awful nightmare.

The conflict threatened our relationship as well—we were so very different. The stress became unbearable. Sometimes we hurt each other expecting too much. We'd misunderstand a word, a glance, a gesture that had different meanings for each of us. Would our love survive?

So when Mahmoud suggested a puppy for my birthday, the gift meant everything. In his homeland, dogs were considered dirty, dangerous creatures suitable only for outdoor guard duty.

Inviting a dog into our home meant Mahmoud understood me. That he wanted me to be happy. And that he knew what would help me most during the most frightening and challenging time of our lives.

Our new German shepherd puppy kept me company when Mahmoud worked nights. We named him Fafnir, after a character in a German opera. Fafnir listened when I worried out loud, clowned to make me laugh, howled when I sang Christmas songs, and licked away my tears—and there were many tears. I missed my distant Indiana family. I felt out of place in the small eastern Kentucky town. I struggled to be a "perfect" wife, and of course failed miserably.

But Fafnir made me feel important. He didn't care if meals never tasted like Mom used to make, he never called me a Yankee, and we seemed to have a common language that needed no words. He thought I was wonderful—and I knew he was special too.

Then Mahmoud was laid off, so that August we moved to Louisville, where he attended graduate school. Less than a week after the move, I found a position as a veterinary assistant. As a special bonus, I could take Fafnir with me to work. Our neighbor's small cockapoo, Fidget, became best buddies with Fafnir. Things were looking up.

Then Fafnir developed a limp. He favored first one paw, and then another. Medicine temporarily relieved his limping, but his paws turned red, itchy, and swollen. He scratched constantly and only seemed happy when playing tag with Fidget.

I tried everything. Antibiotics made him sick. A special diet didn't help, and his weight dropped to fifty-nine pounds. Despite my discount, treatment costs added up and up—never good for newlyweds, and especially difficult with Christmas around the corner.

Nothing seemed to help. Fafnir was allergic to the air he breathed—the molds, pollens, and other allergens of the Ohio Valley region. We cleaned the carpet, tossed out holiday candles, and even got rid of the Christmas tree, thinking that might make a difference. But as the holidays approached, his condition grew worse day by day.

Fafnir always loved visiting the clinic because of all the friends—human and furred—he made. But now, pet owners shrank away and pulled their dogs out of nose-sniffing range. They didn't want Fafnir to give his "horrible disease" to their beloved pets. Although he wasn't contagious, I couldn't blame people for their concern. Fidget still invited games, but Fafnir could no longer play. He hurt too much.

Fafnir had lost so much fur, he no longer looked like a German shepherd. His once expressive ears were naked on the outside, the tender inside sore with angry-looking scabs. Constant licking and chewing stained his tummy black. He limped like an aged, arthritic canine. And he smelled.

He was only fourteen months old.

Had love blinded my eyes and my logic? If this poor creature belonged to somebody else, would I also shrink from touching the affectionate dog? How could I justify continued treatment? Was there a better, more compassionate option?

No! Not my Fafnir! I veered away from the thought before it fully formed, but a smaller voice of reason insisted I face the facts and realities of the dog's condition. Was I being selfish? Would death be the kindest treatment of all?

I couldn't bother Mahmoud with the question—he had enough to worry about with his studies. Besides, Fafnir belonged heart and soul to me, and this awful choice had to be mine alone. For two days and nights I argued with myself, one moment sure that any life was better than an early separation from my beloved dog, the next trying to find strength within myself to stop his suffering.

The third morning, driving the short distance to work, I could hardly see the street through my tear-clouded eyes. Fafnir licked my neck, excited as always to visit the clinic and see his friends. Maybe he'd get to sniff a cat (oh doggy joy!).

The busy morning moved quickly from case to case while Fafnir rested in his usual kennel. Each time I dug into my pocket for suture scissors or a pen and touched the crumpled paper, my eyes filled again. It was the euthanasia authorization form I'd decided to complete during lunch break after playing with Fafnir one last time.

Then an emergency case arrived. A young woman, nearly hysterical with fear, carried a Pomeranian puppy into the clinic. "It's Foxy, please help! He chewed through an electrical cord on the Christmas tree." The woman's two young children watched with wide, tearful eyes.

The veterinarian began immediate treatment. "A transfusion would help since the pup's in shock. Lucky we have Fafnir here as a donor."

At the time, veterinary clinics needing donors often drew blood from their staff members' own large dogs. In exchange for being on call, Fafnir received discounted services. I wasn't surprised when she assumed Fafnir would give blood because he'd been a donor dog for some time. The idea Fafnir might save Foxy on the last day of his own life shocked me.

I froze. For an endless moment I couldn't breathe. Then without a word, I brought my boy out of the kennel. His eyes lit up at the chance to sniff Foxy's small, shivering body. Fafnir's bald tail waved, and he grinned. I had to coax him away to draw twelve cc's of precious blood from his foreleg to be given to his tiny new friend. He might look sick on the outside, but Fafnir's blood was perfectly healthy.

By lunchtime, Foxy's gums transformed from white to a healthy pink, and he breathed normally. The red puppy even managed a feeble wag and sniffed back when Fafnir nosed him through the kennel bars.

For the first time in three days, I could smile through what had become happy tears. Without looking at it, I pulled the euthanasia paper from my pocket, crumpled it up, and tossed it into the trash. What if I'd made that decision even an hour earlier? If Fafnir hadn't been there for Foxy, the puppy would have died.

Fafnir grinned up at me, and I realized he didn't care how he looked. Fafnir patiently put up with the unknowns in his world, with uncomfortable baths, bitter pills, and scary needle sticks he couldn't control, simply because he loved and trusted me to keep him safe. Fafnir willingly came to Foxy's rescue, just as he'd rescued me during the first troubled months of my marriage. That's what we do for our friends, for the ones we love. Sometimes we rescue strangers too, simply because it brings such joy.

Mahmoud never blinked over the extra medical expenses for Fafnir, and that made me love him even more. Six months later, Mahmoud attained his master's degree and found a great job, and we moved from Louisville to Tennessee. Away from the allergens that had plagued him, Fafnir quickly recovered and no longer needed medication. My heart swelled with quiet thanks during each afternoon walk when neighbors admired Fafnir's proud stride and glowing coat and begged to pet him.

In Tennessee, I began to write about my experiences working at the vet's office. My first published article told Fafnir's story of his Christmas gift to a tiny red puppy and launched my pet writing career. Today, I now understand how human stress impacts our pets' health, so it makes sense the challenges Mahmoud and I faced were reflected in Fafnir's health.

Fafnir has been my furry muse ever since and will forever live on in my heart and the writerly work he inspired. He—and the furry wonders we've loved since—turned Mahmoud into a passionate pet advocate as well. More than that, Fafnir's infectious grin, his quiet trust, and his delight at meeting new critters (looky, a cat!) fill the pages of my heart with a joy beyond words.

5

Daddy's Dogma

Andi Lehman

When my childhood dog passed away unexpectedly, I left my office in Memphis and drove out to the suburbs to be with my parents. A steady November rain on the windshield mirrored my tears. Never again would I have another dog. It hurt so much to say goodbye.

My folks empathized and gave me time to grieve—but only a little. As Thanksgiving approached, Dad met me in town for coffee. Elbows on the table, he sipped the dark liquid and eyed me over the rim of his mug.

"I know you're still sad," he said. "Have you considered getting a puppy?"

I shook my head. "No, Daddy. Even if I wanted to, it's way too soon to think about another dog."

He pooched out his lips before imparting the unsolicited advice I assumed would follow. "The best cure," he said, "for the pain of losing a cherished pet is a new pet. The greatest tribute you can pay an animal you loved and lost is to love another."

I poured some cream into my coffee cup and watched the swirling white shape infuse the brown brew like a ghostly embrace.

"Well, that may be," I said. "But I'm not ready."

Dad let it go, but he didn't give up.

On Thanksgiving Day, Dad broached the subject again after dinner. I sat on the maroon leather couch in the den, and Dad lounged in his big recliner. On his lap, he balanced a bowl of his favorite dessert, cherry pie topped with vanilla ice cream.

"Zip," he said between bites, calling me by my family nickname, "I met the perfect dog for you in a customer's office this week. Cutest thing I ever saw—a white ball of fluff sitting under her desk."

I swallowed a mouthful of my mother's sweet roasted pecans before I yielded to my curiosity. "What kind of dog?"

My father's spoon hung in midair as he gave me a sly look. "I don't know. I'll ask my client next week."

"Well, just remember," I said, "I'm not in the market for one."

A week later, Dad called me at work, a practice normally reserved for urgent news or circumstances.

"Hi, Zippy, it's not an emergency, but I wanted to call you before I forget."

I sighed. My father never forgot anything. He ploughed ahead with his purpose.

"I asked about that little dog. It came from a local breeder."

Despite my annoyance, I swallowed the worm he dangled. "What breed was it?"

He cleared his throat as if to make a profound announcement. "It's a toy poodle," he said.

I thought I'd misheard him. "A *poodle*?"

In an instant, I pictured a barking diva-dog with puff balls of fur at all ends. How could my macho, military father possibly think that a prissy poodle was the perfect dog for me, his oldest tomboy daughter? I tried to close the subject forever.

"I don't want another dog, Daddy, especially not a poodle. I appreciate your concern, I really do, but please, stop badgering me."

For the next two weeks, the holidays kept me busy with social engagements and work functions. The weekend before Christmas, I drove home with some packages to put under the tree. My dad greeted me at the door. He took the bright boxes and deposited them on the kitchen table.

"Perfect timing," he said as he hugged me. "I was just going to see the poodle breeder about a Christmas present."

I pulled away and tossed my purse on the kitchen counter. Would the man never give up? I took a deep breath and spoke in a slow and steady voice, the one I used for misbehaving children when I babysat.

"Dad. I told you. I am not interested in a puppy. And when I'm ready—if I'm ever ready—I will pick it out and pay for it myself."

He never missed a beat. He lifted his arms, palms out, in a hands-off gesture and beamed a cherubic smile at me.

"Who said it was for you?" he asked. "I'm thinking about getting another pet for your mother and me."

I felt my suspicion meter fluctuate for a moment. Could this be true? My parents already had a dog, a big slobbery basset hound named Moose whom they inherited when my brother went to college. As I considered the verity of his last statement, my dad added another salient point. If he bought a puppy, he would need someone to hold it while he drove home.

I started to suggest several options. A cardboard box or a laundry basket might serve as a carrier. Perhaps my mom or my younger sister could accompany him. Better them than me.

Like a master chess player anticipating my moves, Dad informed me that the other women had gone shopping. And besides, he wanted to surprise my mother. He just needed me to keep an eye on the pup during the return trip. He added that it wouldn't take long—he knew what he wanted.

While we drove, Dad chatted away like a merry elf. For nearly an hour, he talked about any subject except our destination. We pulled into a gravel driveway and followed it to a modest ranch house at the end of the lane. From the kennels in the back of the dwelling, a choir of off-key howlers greeted us.

When we stepped into the breeder's living room, the sight overwhelmed me. Dogs lay everywhere, on the furniture, the floors, even the doormats. Big ones and little ones, purebreds and mixed mutts, they fixed their eyes on us and wagged their tails nonstop. The energy from their collective tails could have powered a windmill.

The genial poodle breeder swished a group of Yorkies, which she also bred, from a couple of chairs. We declined her invitation to sit. Dad introduced himself and me and said he came to see the litter of beautiful poodles she had mentioned over the phone. As she bustled out to fetch them, I rolled my eyes at him. He winked back. I shook my head in exasperation. Why butter up the breeder like a piece of toast?

But I melted when I saw her puppies. She brought them out two at a time, one tiny bundle in each fist. The first were solid black roly-poly scamps full of energy and bounce. Forgetting my protestations, I got down on the carpet to pet them. They bowled over one another, ignoring me except when they ran into my legs. Their fur, when they stopped moving long enough for me to touch it, felt soft and fine. And it was all one length—no poofs in sight. The pups looked more like tiny black lambs than my imaginary manicured poodles.

The breeder brought us two more, both apricot-colored, and they tumbled along after the others, yapping at their siblings. I looked at my dad. How would he ever choose? He studied the puppies from his six-foot-four height. He seemed disappointed.

"Is this all you have?" he asked.

The owner considered us for a long moment. We must have passed her evaluation.

"I do have a second smaller litter, but they just turned six weeks old, younger than I normally sell them. And none of them has been shown yet, so they may be shy. I'll bring them out for you."

She returned with a trio of white puppies in her hands and set them gently on the rug. Two of them joined the yipping fray and wobbled on stubby limbs toward the slightly larger puppies already on the ground. The third sat immobile, like a wise and silent baby owl, right where the woman deposited him.

His fur was thick and full and begged to be stroked. It curled down on either side of his black nose like a wide handlebar moustache, giving him a jaunty, manly air. He tipped his head to the left and blinked at us through dark, sleepy eyes.

My dad didn't hesitate. "I'll take that one," he said.

I looked up from the floor to question his judgment. The quiet fellow seemed so introverted compared to the others. But Daddy reached into his pocket for his checkbook and pen. He handed his payment to the startled woman, who wisely stifled her opinion. Bending toward the writhing canine mass for the first time, Dad scooped the plump puppy into one of his big hands and looked squarely into the tiny face. Then he thanked the breeder, marched out to the van, and handed the adorable creature to me trailing behind him.

As we pulled out of the driveway and headed for home, I cradled the little dog to my chest and pushed the tips of my fingers into the deep white coat. My dad never said a word, and the puppy had yet to make a sound, not one whine. He licked my face gently. The scent of sweet puppy breath lingered on my chin.

I glared at my father, now also looking a bit owl-like, self-satisfied, and serene. He kept his gaze on the road ahead, but the corners of his lips twitched. He waited for me to acknowledge the power of a persistent parent and a two-pound poodle. I buried my nose in soft, silky fur and gave my dad his due. In a muffled voice, I admitted my defeat.

"Okay," I said. "How much do I owe you?"

When we got home, my mom and sister, aware of the trip and sure of the outcome, never even bothered to feign surprise. They admired my new furry charge and congratulated my dad, who took a moment to bask in their compliments. Now that he had coerced me into getting a puppy, he proceeded to name it as well.

"A little dog needs a big moniker," he said. "You should call him Rhett Butler."

I attempted to hold my own by suggesting a few alternatives like James Bond or Popcorn, but Dad's choice prevailed. And before the week's end, my Rhett was as charming and rascally as his namesake. Endlessly curious, he raised a playful paw to every living thing he met. He explored his surroundings with busy abandon until he grew tired and collapsed on the spot for a quick, regenerative snooze. I orbited around him like a protective mother moon, adoring him just as my father predicted.

On Christmas day, I woke up in my childhood bed with my diminutive companion snuggled next to me on the comforter. That morning our family knew nothing of the joys and adventures that lay ahead with Rhett Butler, nor could we know we would mourn the passing of my dad before we said goodbye to the toy poodle that he chose for me. But as Rhett played under the Christmas tree, chasing wrapping-paper balls and tugging on the old basset hound's ears, I recognized the wisdom in my father's tenet. It would bear repeating through the decades of delightful dogs who blessed my life.

The surest remedy for the loss of a cherished pet is another pet. A wounded heart heals best when it loves again.

6

Early Christmas Surprise

Loretta Eidson

W here did she go?" I muttered as I walked outside in the blustery wind to look for our very pregnant golden retriever, Casey. "Brrr." The damp air and low temperatures from last night's downpour sent a chill over me. I whistled and called out to her again.

Dark gray clouds blanketed the sky, and the weatherman had predicted freezing rain, sleet, and snow. I traipsed back inside and grabbed a jacket. Any other day, I'd send one of my three kids out to see about her, but they were at school, their last day before Christmas break.

They'd begged for a dog two years ago and promised to take care of her. After much deliberation and angst, I relented and agreed. She was their dog.

I had known nothing about dogs. I grew up with a goldfish. It didn't jump on me, lick me, run around my feet playfully, or bark. All I had to do was feed it and clean out the fishbowl. My mother didn't like cats, and my little sister was afraid of dogs, so I never owned a four-legged pet. Until now.

Today I found myself worried about Casey. She was an affectionate, smart, and even-tempered dog. Her silky reddish coat, floppy ears, and trusting eyes added to her beauty. She loved playing and rolling in the yard with the kids. Any time the back door opened, she came running with her tail wagging. But today, she hadn't made her presence known.

Wouldn't you know, the moment I stepped into the yard, another downpour began? Freezing rain and sleet hit my face, sending me back inside for an umbrella. I shook my head, frustrated that I was home alone and had to tend to the dog. Carey, my oldest son, always arrived home from school before his younger siblings, and his school bus would arrive in thirty minutes. What if I waited and let him search the yard? No, my heart wouldn't let it go. An urgency welled up inside me. I had to see what kept her from responding.

Out I went. The umbrella protected my hair and helped keep my makeup intact, but from the waist down, my clothes became soaked. I stepped in a mudhole just as a burst of wind threatened to yank the umbrella from my grip.

I trudged toward the back of our property, where a large drainage ditch, half full of rushing water, threatened more erosion. Several holes stretched along the chain-link fence that divided our yard from the trench. Some holes were small and some bigger. It was apparent Casey had dug a few more.

"Casey, come here, girl. Where are you?" I kept calling her name and walking the fence line.

I drew closer to the corner of the yard next to the ditch. There was Casey, her ears perked up. She lay, soaked and shivering, in a large hole. "Hey, girl." I moved closer, wondering why she wasn't offering to come to me. Was she stuck?

The instant I stood over her and looked down, compassion filled my heart. She'd given birth to eight beautiful puppies out in the frigid weather. She looked up at me with pleading eyes. At least, that's the way I read them. Would her babies be swept under the fence and washed down into the ditch? I couldn't leave her.

Without another thought, I squatted, reached out, and held the umbrella over her and her pups, exposing myself to the weather. I had no other choice, and no one to help me move them. Casey hadn't taken advantage of the soft, warm bed we prepared for her in the storage room. Why this dangerous hole? I didn't understand.

My cell phone lay on the counter in the kitchen, so calling for help wasn't an option. Most of my neighbors worked, which left me to figure out how to resolve the situation. My wet hair lay flat against my head, and water dripped from my chin. I could feel my nonwaterproof mascara streaking my face.

I was determined to hold the umbrella over Casey and her newborns, so my only choice was to stay put and wait for my son's arrival. I switched hands each time my arm grew tired of holding the umbrella straight out in front of me, and the bursts of wind that forced a tighter grip didn't help.

"Hey, girl, you sure picked a risky place to bring babies into the world, but look at you. Eight beautiful little ones. As soon as Carey gets home, we'll get you and your pups inside the storage room where it's dry and warm." I talked, petted her, and rubbed her head.

She kept checking on her babies and licking them. Her tail offered a small wag as she looked up at me with those intelligent eyes and nudged my hand. It was as if she was thanking me for being there.

A loud motor rounded the corner, and brakes screeched. Children's laughter echoed into the backyard. The squeak of the carport gate alerted me my son was home.

"Carey!" I yelled.

"Mom, where are you?"

He ran into the yard, and his eyes met mine. His jaw dropped as he walked toward me with the hood of his jacket covering his head. "You're all wet. What are you doing?"

"Casey had her puppies. We need to move them to the storage room."

I reached into the hole, pulled out one puppy at a time, and handed them to Carey. He held one in each hand and rushed around the corner of the yard. Seconds later, he returned. We repeated the process until the last two puppies were in his hands.

Casey jumped up, dancing alongside my son as they entered the storage room. She checked her pups, nuzzled and licked them, then curled her soaked body around them. Carey sat on the blanket with her, in awe of eight more dogs.

I kicked off my muddy shoes in the carport and darted inside for a towel for the dogs. Carey and I towel-dried Casey's fur and the puppies as best we could. We moved her water and food bowls just outside the storage room door.

Moments later, another school bus stopped in front of our house. Tracy and Clint hopped off and raced up the driveway, but before they reached the carport gate, Carey yelled, "Casey had her puppies!" His smile covered his face, and his siblings squealed.

Snow began blanketing the ground, and the afternoon sky grew darker. The kids came inside long enough to put their books in their rooms before they went back out to pamper Casey and her babies.

I was thankful we'd placed a small heater on the shelf inside the storage room when we prepared for Casey's birthing. My kids and the dogs were safe and warm. A hot shower called out to me, and I succumbed, relieved our beautiful golden retriever and her little ones had weathered the storm.

That cold, wet day, two weeks before Christmas, I bonded with Casey like I never dreamed I would with a dog.

7

Annie Oakley's Holiday Scarf

Lonnie Hull DuPont

My only sister, Peggy, and I grew up loving Christmas, and we continued to enjoy it as adults. She made the holiday a wonderful experience for her kids and then her grandkids, and she made my husband, Joe, and me feel special at Christmas too. He and I didn't usually attend family celebrations on Christmas Eve because Joe ran the soundboard at our church's Christmas Eve service. So during each busy Christmas season, Peggy and her husband, Dick, would set aside one night with only Joe and me at their house, and we would make nachos together. I made guacamole, and because I can't eat beef, Peggy always spoiled me by having a separate Crock-Pot of spicy ground turkey for my nachos—an especially considerate thing since she and Dick ran a cattle ranch. Then the four of us would watch Christmas movies and gab into the night until we couldn't stay awake. It was relaxed and fun.

Peggy and Dick raised longhorns in Michigan. One day they acquired a young Australian cattle dog—a blue heeler. This robust and bright breed of dog is part dingo. They named her Annie Oakley and had her professionally trained for cattle work. But she was also their baby. She was the smartest creature in the room at any time and had a great personality—one of those dogs who makes friends for life with anyone who will play with her. On those wintry Christmas nacho and movie nights, Annie took turns being with each one of us, sitting next to us on the couch or trying to get on our laps, even though she was too big for that. She seemed to enjoy the holiday time together as much as we did.

Over the years, Annie became most attached to my sister. The dog followed her around and responded to her with great affection, and my sister fussed over her in return. Then one day, Peggy went to the emergency room and never came home. She died within a few weeks from previously undiagnosed cancer.

Annie lost her favorite human. Really, we all did. Friends and family would be in shock over this for a long time. But I also worried about the dog.

My brother-in-law and I talked on the phone a few times in the following months. Eventually he let me know that he was so lonely that he was ready to find another woman in his life. I accepted that. I knew about statistics showing that widowed men who had good marriages were likely to find someone new sooner than later. Peggy and Dick had had a good marriage, and he missed that companionship.

Through a dating site for farmers, my brother-in-law met Jan. She was also widowed, and she owned a miniature donkey ranch several miles away. Dick and Jan had a lot in common and became good friends, even doing chores and attending auctions together. She was a very nice and interesting woman, and I liked her as soon as I met her—which was on Christmas Eve.

Peggy was my last remaining relative in my immediate family, and I felt bereft after she died. And things changed. Her house was always an open door to me, but it felt different now. I'd known Dick since I was seventeen and considered him my own brother, but the house was more my sister's domain. The change was unnerving for me, so I tended to stay away except for a few hours that first Christmas without Peggy. I was still in too much shock to take it all in.

A year after my sister died, my oldest nephew got married in a lovely ceremony at the ranch. I briefly stopped in at the ranch house the night before the event, the first time since Christmas. As soon as I parked in the driveway, Annie Oakley trotted up to my car. She stood on her hind legs to say hello through the window, but the window height of my Kia Soul and the length of her stretched-out body did not quite match—which meant I could only see her paws on my window and her pointed dingo ears. It was comical and sweet.

I got out of the car and saw Dick in the driveway with Jan. We chatted for a while, then they walked to the barns, and I headed back to my car to go home. As I started my engine, I cast a longing look back at the house, wishing my sister were still there; I missed her so much right then, especially on the eve of her son's wedding. But what I saw made me feel some happiness. Annie was trotting toward the barns behind Jan, right at her heels, in such a way that made me realize that the dog had attached herself to a new friend: Jan. I cannot fully convey how relieved that made me. Annie was going to be all right.

Several months later, I stopped in for a few hours on Christmas Eve. My husband had to work that day, then drive straight to the Christmas Eve service. I skipped church and drove to the ranch by myself. My nephews and their families would be there, and Jan too, for this second holiday without Peggy. When I drove into the driveway, I paused and sat in my car. I was no longer sure which door to go to. I used to go through the garage, open the door, and holler hello. Things were different now.

Someone opened the back door to let the dog out, and when Annie saw my car, she galloped my way. Again, she stood on her hind legs and I could only see her front paws and pointed ears. But she was my sturdy little welcomer.

I followed her indoors and said my hellos. Annie was clearly in her element around all these people. She was a very social dog, making the rounds for attention. Then I realized she was wearing a Christmas scarf, full of holiday colors. Now ordinarily I might not think much of a cattle dog in a scarf. She was a rough-and-tumble little girl, aptly named Annie Oakley, and this was not unlike forcing a tomboy into a prom dress. But she seemed okay with it.

"I like Annie's scarf," I told Jan, though to be honest, I was being polite.

"Annie likes scarves," Jan responded, dead serious. "She has several. She doesn't like wearing a hat, but she likes wearing a scarf."

I considered that. It certainly seemed to be so.

But it really was something else. Annie was fine wearing a scarf because *Jan* dressed her up—and Annie clearly adored Jan. That made me happy all over again. It helped me relax and have a nice Christmas Eve with Annie and the humans.

It may seem strange to say that watching Annie process change after losing Peggy helped me do the same. But it's true. I miss my sister, and things will never be the same, especially at Christmas. But if Annie can adjust, so can I. If Annie Oakley can enjoy Christmas again, I can too.

8

The Dog Days of Winter

Susan C. Willett

In December, my neighborhood fills with multicolor displays of Christmas lights and Hanukkah menorahs glowing in the windows. Morning frost limns the grass and fallen leaves with outlines of thin silver. Scarves and hats and gloves are pulled from the basket on the top shelf of the closet. But the snow boots sit untouched, waiting for the right combination of cold and moisture to deliver winter's first snowfall.

Every year I wonder if my three dogs remember what snow is like. It could have been as long as nine or ten months since they last experienced it back in February or March here in New Jersey. But I should know better. Because every year, when I open the back door onto our deck and yard covered with the white stuff—whether it's the first snowfall or the seventh, if it's knee-deep or if you can still see the grass sticking out like a stubbled beard—the dogs bound out and romp through it with joyous excitement like it's the best thing ever.

Every single year. Every single snowfall.

My long-legged couch-potato hound Jasper dances like a puppy, even at the stately age of ten. His normally dignified border collie mix sister, Lilah—who's the same age, and who tends to take change quite seriously—finds herself with a sudden case of the zoomies. And our middle-aged dog Tucker, our peripatetic terrier, begins a game of chase with a joyful play bow. Snow brings out the puppy in all of them.

The dogs lift their muzzles to the air and leap at the snowflakes. If there's enough on the ground, they run with their mouths low, scooping up the snow, leaving trailing lines and paw prints behind. When it's deep enough, the three pups will help me build a snow person. By "help" I mean digging at the giant snowballs that I roll through the yard to build my creation or borrowing a stick arm for a game of fetch. Sometimes, I'll craft a snow dog—or even a snow cat—and Lilah, Jasper, and Tucker will obediently pose next to the frozen canine or feline, as if it's just another member of the pack.

Snow is fun, but under some circumstances it can cause a few challenges. For example, it's a bit difficult for Lilah and Tucker to walk when the snow is as deep as their shoulders. Jasper doesn't have the same issue; his long legs come in handy when there's a foot and a half of the white stuff covering the ground. In those cases, Jasper will march his way through it, creating a rough path so that the two shorter dogs can follow in his footsteps, quite literally.

Once a path is cleared—after three dogs have trampled their way back and forth on it a few times—Lilah, Jasper, and Tucker use it as a highway, racing through it at top speed.

But sometimes there are doggy reasons to leave the beaten path, to take the route untraveled. There might be a squirrel that needs chasing or a deer in the woods behind our home that must be barked at. Then Lilah may bound through the snow, leaving telltale bounce prints as she jumps toward her destination. Tucker isn't into bouncing, so he just plain pushes his way through, using his chest as a plow.

It's also hard for a dog to do what dogs need to do. Nobody wants to dirty up their snow superhighway, so each of the pups will venture off the path to do their business. Lilah squats quickly and moves on, with a somewhat cold derriere. Tucker always seems to have the most difficult time; it's a challenge to lift a leg if the snow is too deep.

When there's enough snow on the ground, it's even hard for a human to walk. That's when I bring out my snowshoes. With them buckled on my boots, my weight is spread out, enabling me to walk across the top of the snow, sinking down only a few inches instead of high-stepping through knee-deep drifts.

One year, when we had a Dagwood-style snowfall sandwich, with several layers of snow piled on top of each other from multiple consecutive storms, I had to bring out the snowshoes. As I was tromping through our backyard, I heard the unmistakable sound of jingling collars behind me. I turned around and found Jasper and Lilah staying close on my heels, with Tucker joining a few moments later. I was leading a canine parade!

That's when inspiration struck. I decided to forge a special path just for the dogs. Because I felt like being creative, I stomped a huge spiral with a tamped-down space in the center—with Lilah, Jasper, and Tucker following me as I made smaller and smaller circles.

That winter, the dogs made use of their spiral path, eventually making their own shortcut trails crisscrossing it and creating spokes that emanated beyond the borders of my original design. Every year since then, if we get enough snow, I don my snowshoes and stomp intricate paths in my yard for the dogs to run through. I think they've come to expect it.

I'm not an expert with snowshoes by any means. They take a little getting used to. I've learned to alter my gait into a duck-footed waddle, with my feet pointing out slightly so I don't clip or step on one shoe with the other foot. I get out of practice in the spring, summer, and fall, so I tend to be a little klutzy the first few times I wear them.

Which was why, one year, when I was walking through the yard carrying a pile of food scraps for the compost pile in our woods, I somehow got my feet tangled, causing me to trip and splat-land in the snow. Within seconds, all three dogs were gathered around me. *Mom's down!*

As my canine audience watched closely, I took a mental injury inventory. Legs? Working. Arms? Movable. Back? Wrenched but viable. Dignity? Trashed.

They huddled around, questioning me: *Are you okay?*

"I'll be fine if you could get your nose out of my eyeball, Jasper.

"And if you could remove your paws from my coat so I could sit up, Tucker.

"And thank you, Lilah, for ensuring my face is really clean."

It wasn't until I started to move and told them I was okay that Lilah, Jasper, and Tucker turned their attention to the dumped contents of the compost pail I had been carrying. I was quite honored that the dogs waited to see if I was okay before attempting to snarf down the apple peels, potato skins, and moldy bread I had dropped.

Maybe my dogs aren't the Lassie-type hero dogs who know how to run and get help.

But that day as I lay in the snow, in the cold of winter, I could feel the concern, love, and care pour over me from my dogs. And it was warm as a summer's day.

9

Frosty's Christmas Party

Lee Juslin

Every Tuesday morning Frosty, my certified therapy dog, and I visited the residents of Sterling House. I don't know who looked forward to the visits more, Frosty or "her" ladies.

I had gotten Frosty from a nearby breeder who wanted to keep her but was unable to due to family circumstances. Frosty was named because of her milk beard—a white patch under her chin.

When a friend told me about therapy dogs, I knew Frosty, a happy little Scottie who loved people, would be perfect. She liked other dogs, learned quickly, and earned her CGC (Canine Good Citizen) certificate before her first birthday.

This particular cool December Tuesday with bright sunshine was extra special. Frosty was dressed in her custom-made Santa suit instead of her therapy vest. I wore a Christmassy Scottie sweater. It was the day of Frosty's annual holiday party.

A good bit of work and planning went into pulling off the annual party. First, I scoured Walmart and the dollar store for little gift items like soaps, perfumes, candies, and other little things to fill the gift bags Frosty would be "handing out" to the residents.

I also printed little gift cards with a black Scottie adorned with a red collar that looked like Frosty. On each one I wrote "Happy Holidays from Lee and Frosty." Originally, I had wrapped each little gift item in Scottie Christmas paper, but when I saw that unwrapping the little gifts was hard on older hands, I came up with a new idea. I used glittery tissue paper to dress up the gift bags instead.

I had met with the home's volunteer coordinator several weeks earlier to set a date for the party, which would occur after they had put up their Christmas tree and other holiday decorations. The home provided refreshments—punch and cookies. I delivered the gift bags the day before the party so the coordinator could store them in a closet and then bring them out for the party as a surprise.

Like for most folks, December is a very busy month for me. I had to organize the items I would donate to the holiday raffles held by many of the breed rescues I regularly support, organize my own holiday décor at home, and pull together all the items for the party. I also had to take Frosty to the spa the day before so she would be looking her most spiffy self on her special day of hosting. As a result, I hadn't had time to get into the Christmas spirit.

As we pulled out of the drive, I began to feel a sense of excitement enveloping us. It was mostly from Frosty belted into the back seat, looking around eagerly. She knew this was a special day. Maybe we didn't have snow here in the South, but we knew how to celebrate with the best of them. *Part-ee!*

We walked up the steps to Sterling House, Frosty with an extra bounce in her step. The door opened to welcome us in. Seated in the big living room in front of the fireplace that burned cheerily and a Christmas tree that blinked and gleamed were all the residents.

As soon as we stepped in, all eyes turned our way, and I heard, "Here's Frosty," "Oh, good, it's Frosty," and "Look, Frosty has a Santa suit!" Some smiled vaguely at me, but clearly, I was unimportant. I was used to being just Frosty's chauffeur, and that was as it should be in therapy visits. Frosty was the star.

Frosty liked her Santa suit except for the hat. So, we had made a deal: she would wear the hat during the visit, but I would remove it as soon as we left to head home. Frosty sashayed like a little diva into the middle of the circle of residents so they could all admire her in her Santa suit. After all, red is such a good color for a little black Scottie. If she could have given the queen's wave, she surely would have. After walking around and greeting everyone, she settled in front of the fireplace.

I took an empty seat among the residents and some of the staff. I always brought a Christmas story or Christmas poems to read to get the party started. Often I read "The Gift of the Magi" or perhaps the wonderful poem "The Night Before Christmas." This time, however, I had found a poem called "The Boy Who Laughed at Santa Claus" by Ogden Nash. Like all of Mr. Nash's works, it is humorous and quirky. The ladies loved it. If you are not familiar with it, you should check it out.

After we had all laughed about the Ogden Nash poem and talked a bit about Christmas, Frosty again became the center of attention. For anyone who wanted it, I lifted Frosty to sit in their lap. I lifted her because Scotties are not known for jumping abilities, and I didn't want to take a chance that one of her toenails would scratch or get caught in someone's clothing.

I then took pictures of each lady holding Santa Frosty. Some might see this as a kind of reverse Santa visit, but with her luxurious beard and eyebrows, plus her small size, Frosty made a pretty good Santa. Never mind that Frosty couldn't do the ho-ho-ho part.

Usually, for reasons of privacy, I don't take photos of the residents, but Sterling House had agreed to allow these at the party. The reason they were allowed was because I would take them home and use them to make individual holiday cards for each resident. Frosty would then deliver them the next week.

There was no doubt that these cards were treasured. Residents who used walkers would put them in the basket of the walker so they could carry them as they went about the home. It was not unusual to see these cards still in the baskets many months later, often well-worn from being opened and handled.

Next, I helped Frosty distribute the gift bags. The volunteer coordinator had given me a head count, and we had prepared a few extras just in case. The extras went first to residents who couldn't attend and then to staff. The delight of everyone as they received their bags and opened the gifts always warmed our hearts.

The staff rolled out a cart of refreshments. At this point, I had to watch carefully to make sure no one tried to feed Frosty their cookies. Instead, I had some dog cookies in my pocket, and a number of the residents happily fed them to Frosty. I never worried that she would hurt anyone's hand, because as a certified therapy dog, she was always very gentle.

As we all sat talking and happily munching our cookies, I thought briefly about how we were ruining our appetites for lunch. But who cared? After all, this was the Christmas season.

Eventually Frosty and I headed to the door, our hostess duties over and another party of the year in the record books. We looked back. The residents smiled over their gifts. Some were still laughing at the Ogden Nash poem, and some were waving. I heard, "Thanks, Frosty" and "See you next week, Frosty."

I felt the Christmas spirit right there in the living room of the home with all our friends smiling and waving. I'm sure Frosty felt it too, and it was spelled l-o-v-e.

10

Perfect

Sherri Gallagher

As a kid I would watch television at Christmas and see families dressed in their finest clothes, gathering around a well-filled table, with beautiful china, lit candles, and sparkling silverware. A mother would hug a daughter and a father would carry on a friendly conversation with a son. The setting would be peaceful, with a lovely tree decked in garlands, ornaments, and tinsel. If grandparents were there, they beamed with love. Like many people, however, I grew up in a household where Christmas was a time of stress, arguments, and hurt feelings and nothing like the perfect Christmases portrayed on the silver screen.

Christmas day was spent rushing between grandparents' houses with the requirement to eat a full dinner at each location. I was a small eater, and no matter how tasty and nutritious the food, large portions upset my stomach. I didn't want to hurt my grandmother's feelings, so I would slip half my dinner to the dog, who waited quietly under the table. Then I would request seconds in a vain attempt to appease my grandmother.

Then we would visit the second set of grandparents, where I was expected to eat again barely an hour after consuming a large meal. I often wished I could box up those delicious meals and send them to the poor starving children in other countries who my grandmother said would be more than happy to have what I left on my plate.

We never had a big Christmas at home. Mom and Dad grabbed a tree from a nearby lot a few days before Christmas. Our tree was decorated quickly; the kids had to stay out of the way so one more task could be swiftly completed. It always felt like a rush to make it through the season—more like a checklist than a celebration. On December twenty-sixth the ornaments were removed and stored, and the tree was hauled to the burn pile. Sister and I were put to work for the day cleaning up any sign of the season past.

Mom and Dad tried to give us nice gifts. One year, Dad made a dollhouse that was a scale model of the house we lived in. On another bitterly cold Christmas Eve, I remember my parents bringing a litter of puppies in from the kennel (Dad bred German shepherds) to keep them safe and warm and give us the fun of chasing puppies and playing tug with scraps of ribbon. So the thing I wanted at Christmas was to stay home and play with our dogs and my new toys.

When I became a new bride, I was determined to change the paradigm of my childhood Christmases. I sat down with my parents and my in-laws separately to set the limits. One of them would get us for Christmas Eve and one for Christmas morning. If they wished for more time with us, they were welcome to join us at our home for Christmas dinner. The plan fit nicely for them, especially since all their parents were no longer with us.

My in-laws had always celebrated Christmas Eve together. This gave my parents Christmas Eve to themselves, the morning with my new husband and me, and the evening with my sister's family. Satisfied I had broken the negative pattern, I was determined to make our first Christmas together a perfect one. I especially wanted the perfect Christmas tree, carefully selected and lovingly decorated.

I had not planned on the devastation an Afghan puppy can create.

A month after our wedding and two months before Christmas, my husband mentioned he had always wanted an Afghan hound. My mother-in-law had a bad experience with dogs as a girl and hadn't allowed her sons to have any pets. I went on a quest to find an Afghan puppy for him. We answered an advertisement for a single puppy. The seller owned the father of the litter and had selected this puppy in payment for the breeding.

The breeder explained that her line of Afghan hounds made instant judgments about people, and they were right 99 percent of the time. She warned us, if the puppy's father didn't like us, we were going home empty-handed.

A few hours later, we were invited to sit in the living room, and my husband selected a bean bag chair. The breeder froze for an instant. Before she could say a word, the puppy's father, Natek, walked in and proceeded to climb into my husband's lap.

The breeder found her voice. "You're sitting in Natek's chair."

My husband smiled and stroked the dog's long silky coat. "I don't mind."

"That's just it—Natek usually *does* mind and removes most people from his spot. He's not a terribly friendly dog."

The breeder brought us the puppy, and we got along splendidly. A few hours later we were driving home with our new family member in my arms. Little did I know my education in hounds was about to begin. At the time I didn't think a thing about the differences between hounds and the herding dogs I grew up with. After all, a dog was a dog, wasn't it?

German shepherds like to please their handlers. Afghan hounds expect their handlers to work to please them. We named the puppy Khan, which means "king," and it fit his attitude. If I had tossed a ball for a German shepherd, she would have raced to fetch it back to me. If I tossed a ball for Khan, he gave me a look that clearly communicated, *You threw it; you go get it.*

Khan believed in returning punishment. If you corrected him for chewing up shoes, peeing on the carpet, or stealing food off the counter, beware. The next time you did something he didn't like, he would deliberately perform every act for which he had ever received a correction.

Prior to Khan joining the family, we had been adopted by a stray kitten. He arrived one day at my husband's shop, flea- and worm-infested and so starved he gladly munched on leftover French fries. We cleaned him up, addressed his medical issues, and named him Fenster. Fenster and Khan became buddies. While we were at work, the two of them would have the run of the house, playing and entertaining themselves, much to the destruction of our furniture, plants, and clothing.

As Christmas approached, I blithely went about decorating, never thinking that a Christmas tree could be a problem. For our first Christmas together, I was determined everything would be "perfect." My husband and I went to a friend's farm to cut down a tree and hauled it home. Our ornaments were a few old glass bulbs we found in a thrift store. Our big splurge was for three strands of twinkle lights, but after that we couldn't afford even tinsel. I made garlands of popcorn and cranberries only to find Khan eating them off the thread faster than I could string them.

My husband and I had a wonderful, romantic evening, hanging lights and ornaments and sipping hot chocolate while eating marshmallows and the occasional handful of popcorn. The house was filled with pine scent, and the twinkle lights gave off the perfect level of illumination. Combined with a fire blazing in the fireplace, it was a Norman Rockwell picture.

Fenster and Khan lounged on the couch, watching us carefully select one of our few bulbs and discuss the exact best spot for it on the tree. As we were finishing the decorations and I was packing away boxes, Fenster approached a low-hanging glass bulb. He sat for a solid minute staring at the reflective surface.

I turned to my husband in delight. "People who say animals can't appreciate beauty have never seen Fenster."

Fenster chose that exact moment to whack the bulb with his front paw and send it flying across the room to smash into the wall. It should have been a sign. Or rather it was a sign, I just didn't recognize it as such.

Afghan hounds are tall dogs with heads capable of cruising a dining room table without the dog jumping up. Even though Khan was a puppy, his long legs and neck put any ornament below three feet from the floor at risk. Now the pine cones I had strung together with ribbon to decorate the fireplace became scattered brown pieces with an occasional bit of gnawed red satin. The single ribbon I had strung on the stair railing hung in limp one- to two-foot lengths with the tips well chewed. Carefully wrapped presents placed under the tree were swiftly unwrapped and the boxes shredded.

Without other dogs to emulate, Khan apparently thought he was a cat. He would bat at ornaments with his front paws until they flew off the tree. He would ignore the fallen orb and look for a new bauble to bat. The tree got top heavy as what few ornaments we could rescue were moved above dog height. The tree was far from the perfection I'd dreamed of with the bottom half clothed only in lights and partially nibbled popcorn garland drooping in odd loops. Our dismal tree made me wonder if there was such a thing as a pleasant Christmas.

The water in the tree stand became Khan's drinking fountain. No matter how much clean, fresh water was in his bowl, Khan preferred the stale water under the tree. That generally left a puddle on the carpet. I consoled myself that the puddle wasn't yellow and from the other end of the dog.

That wasn't the worst of it. Each night when we came home from work, we would find the tree canted over at strange angles or outright toppled with more of the garland consumed. We were at a loss as to how it was happening since both Fenster and Khan would be dozing on the sofa when we got home. They would race to the door to greet us, but their half-asleep eyes and warm fur made it clear we had awakened them from naps.

We speculated that Khan, dining on the garland, pulled the pine tree over. But when we tested that theory by pulling on the garland ourselves, we simply broke the thread, and kernels scattered on the floor. Khan raised his head from the sofa but otherwise didn't react. Fenster, on the other hand, quickly gobbled up the scattered popcorn.

My husband suggested our pets were knocking the tree askew during one of their daily games of tag. Fenster was not a big cat and Khan didn't weigh twenty pounds. There was no way even if they worked together that they could push over the tree, but no other explanation made sense. We addressed our theory by tightening the screws that held the tree upright in the base and moving the tree closer to the wall and out of the traffic pattern. It still wasn't enough. Each night we would right the tree and clean up broken ornaments and speculate as to what mischief had caused our Christmas tree to lean at crazy angles.

It was Christmas Eve before we finally got our answer. I had worked all morning preparing a turkey, candied yams, and apple and cherry pies. The house was filled with wonderful scents of the baking bird and sweet breads, all underlaid with the tang of pine from our bedraggled tree. I was cleaning the living room in preparation for my in-laws joining us when Fenster and Khan engaged in a rousing game of tag, barely missing me as they romped by. The cat would chase the dog and then they would switch, and Khan would chase Fenster. It was truly entertaining to watch and had me laughing. That is, until Fenster raced up the tree and Khan followed.

It was a perfect lesson in the physics of a pendulum. A small dog and cat on the bottom of the tree had no impact but as they climbed, their combined weight at the top of the trunk swayed the tree precariously to the side until it was so far over Khan toppled out of the branches, taking several ornaments with him. Fenster's claws kept him anchored in the branches, at least until Khan was on the ground. At that point Fenster leaped to land on the dog, and they took off running again while I stood in the wreckage of our last few ornaments and burst into tears. Any chance of a perfect Christmas tree was ruined. All our ornaments were destroyed, and my in-laws were due to arrive shortly.

My husband appeared with an armful of firewood, bringing indoors the bite and smell of cold winter air. He dumped his burden on the hearth, collected me into his arms, and tried to coax an explanation out of me.

Between sobs and hiccups, I explained. As I surveyed the damage, the fountain of tears opened back up into a gusher, and I sobbed, "It's all ruined. Your mother is going to think I'm an awful wife who doesn't care enough to make Christmas special. She'll say you should have found a different wife. I wanted our first Christmas to be different from what I grew up with. I wanted this Christmas to be perfect and to finally have a perfect tree. Now everything is ruined. There's no hope of having a nice Christmas."

Credit my husband for not laughing. Instead, he stroked my hair. "My mom isn't going to think a bit of that. She was sure I would be a bachelor forever, and she's very grateful I found someone willing to marry me."

Unconvinced, I moved away to wipe my eyes and blow my nose. Surveying the damage and the mess, I almost fled back to hide in my husband's arms. We had little more than an hour before our guests would arrive. The tree lay on its side with several broken branches creating a flat spot. The glass ornaments were a kaleidoscope of fragments, and what little garland remained had slithered up the tree to wrap the top like a full-belled skirt with the wearer doing a handstand.

"You finish the cleaning and the cooking. I'll take care of the tree."

"You might as well chop it up for firewood," I whined.

"Trust me. I've got this." He grinned.

I finished sweeping and dusting and returned to the kitchen to set the table, full of trepidation as to what my new in-laws would think and reliving previous Christmases with my grandparents. My husband appeared in the kitchen once to borrow some aluminum foil and commandeer my leftover cranberries.

A knock came on the door before I could check on his handiwork. I collected coats, and my husband ushered his mother into the living room. As I hung the garments in the closet, I heard her exclaim, "What a beautiful tree. And look at those sweet creatures enjoying it."

Curious—and more than a little suspicious my mother-in-law was either being overly kind or deeply sarcastic—I slipped into the back of the room. She was right. My husband had returned the tree to vertical, fitted the crushed side against the wall, and wired the top to the ceiling. He'd decorated the wires with aluminum foil and strategically placed light strands, so they looked like glowing streamers from the star on the top. He'd repaired the garland and filled the empty spaces with clusters of cranberries. To top things off, he'd cut out cardboard stars, covered them in foil, and spaced them around to act as ornaments. Khan and Fenster, tired from their afternoon exercise, were asleep under the tree in the dog bed we had purchased for them as a Christmas gift. It was a picture-perfect Norman Rockwell moment.

The rest of the evening went exactly as I'd dreamed it would. The dinner drew rave reviews, with more than enough for everyone. Gifts were unwrapped with all the appropriate exclamations. Khan and Fenster entertained everyone by playing and pouncing in the discarded wrapping paper. My mother-in-law overcame her terror of dogs when Khan climbed into her lap and proceeded to go to sleep between one breath and the next.

I finally learned that perfect can happen even when things don't go as planned. I finally had my perfect Christmas.

11

Christmas in December, Christmas in July

Mary C. Busha

Little would my husband, Bob, and I have guessed that as a result of a violent windstorm, we would eventually be blessed beyond measure. But that's what happened, for the storm began a series of events that dropped into our home—not literally, of course—a sweet little dog who would be a Christmas present we will never forget.

While America's southeast is famous for its storms, this was the first hurricane Bob and I had experienced since our move from Michigan to Florida just two years prior. Before and leading up to Hurricane Irma's landfall in September 2017, we were invited to seek shelter in Georgia. But since several widows lived in our cul-de-sac, and because my son's family, just twenty minutes away, planned to shelter in place, we decided to remain in town.

Now those familiar with hurricane zones know that sometimes residents have a week or more to prepare. But for older women on their own, that can be difficult, if not downright scary. So Bob and I took it upon ourselves to call on the ladies several times before the actual storm to be sure they had what they needed. By and far, being longtime Florida residents, they were fine. But I was glad to check on them and get to know them better. That's when I met Molly, a longtime shih tzu companion of one of the ladies. Because of failing health, Molly's human could no longer walk her dog.

I had been wanting a dog. More like aching for a dog. Our first and only pet in our twenty-seven years of marriage was our little guy Scruffy, who we needed to rehome due to some lifestyle changes. We found a loving home for him, but I never really got over Scruffy.

It seemed until we moved to our home in Florida that the timing was never right to have another dog. Now, after all these years, Bob and I began discussing the possibility. But where to begin? The county animal shelter? The humane society? Online searches? We tried them all, but to no avail. I think I was looking for another Scruffy. I think in a way Bob was too.

We became frustrated. And since obtaining a new pet was not a subject to be taken lightly, Bob suggested, "If God wants us to have another dog, the dog is going to have to come up to our front door and ring the doorbell. Then we'll be sure it's the right one and the right thing to do." In other words, it would have to be an unusual set of circumstances, something out of the ordinary, something divinely arranged.

I prayed that if another dog was *not* to be ours, my longing would lessen. It never did, so I knew one was coming our way, but I would have to be still until it happened.

In the meantime, I had an idea. *What if I contact Molly's owner to see if I can take Molly for morning walks?* I certainly needed the exercise, and Molly did too. Both my neighbor and Molly were pleased at my offer. Every morning for several weeks, my new exercise partner waited for me around 7:30 to walk up the drive to her house and knock on her door.

By now, most households and businesses were back to normal following the storm. But there were some aftereffects. In early October, our newspaper reported the discovery of a dog hoarding situation with fifty-six dogs. The authorities rescued the dogs, most of them miniature poodles who previously had been part of a puppy mill, and took them to the county shelter. Photos of these dogs being taken from the home showed them matted and mangy, frightened and sickly. One report said that within about six weeks, they would have all the dogs cleaned up, vaccinated, spayed or neutered, and ready for adoption. I remember saying, "I don't think so."

Molly and I continued our walks. One morning as we passed a new neighbor working outside, we stopped to say hello. The man complimented me on Molly. I told him she was not mine, but that I walked Molly because her owner was not able to do so. I added, "We do want a dog of our own, however, when the time is right."

"Are you looking?" he asked.

I said, "Sorta." I didn't want to go into the whole dog-coming-to-the-door-and-ringing-the-doorbell thing.

The man suggested we stop by and see Dr. Ed, the veterinarian about two miles from our home. "Sometimes vets know about dogs who need homes." I thanked him for the suggestion and continued my walk with Molly. When I got home, I told Bob what our neighbor had mentioned.

We didn't stop by Dr. Ed's office right away, but about a week later, almost on a whim, Bob said, "Hey, do you want to drop by the vet's office?"

"Well, sure." I wasn't going to protest.

We entered Dr. Ed's office, and when the customer in front of us stepped aside to wait for an order, we introduced ourselves to the receptionist and told her why we were there. She told us she didn't know of any dog needing a home but would be happy to take our names and numbers.

Then the customer who had stepped aside said, "I didn't mean to be listening to your conversation, but my wife and I foster dogs, and right now we have two small dogs. One's a Jack Russell and the other is a little poodle. If you'd like to see them, you'll need to contact the local SPCA and make arrangements to come over."

As soon as we got home, Bob made the call, and the next morning we were at the couple's home. The Jack Russell greeted us at the door with the man and his wife. While the dog was cute, we didn't feel drawn to him, so I asked, "Did you say you also had a poodle?"

"Oh, right, Daisy's in our room," the lady said. "All she does is sit in her crate and whine. But you can see her if you want to." She began to tell us about this little dog. "She was one of fifty-six dogs rescued by the county in October." I told her that we knew the story well. Apparently, this lady had adopted two of the poodles, one for her daughter in another state and one to keep. She was willing to let this one go since she just stayed in her crate. I wasn't interested in obtaining the dog, but I was curious to see her.

Now I'm a list maker, so prior to us looking, I had listed the qualities I wanted in a dog: female, small to medium, non-shedding, fuzzy-wuzzy, and does not smell like a dog. All those, except female, fit our Scruffy, so I knew there were dogs like that. Well, the little dog in the crate fit my list—except she was not fuzzy. She and all the other hoarded dogs had been shaved to the skin because of all the matting. She was not pretty at all. And I was ready to leave.

Bob, however, sat down on the floor and began to coax the little girl out of the crate. "Come on, puppy; it's okay, come on." And slowly she moved to the door of the crate and then out on the carpet and then over to where Bob sat. He picked her up and held her close. He whispered in her ear, and all the while, I was standing there thinking, *This is definitely not the one.*

The lady invited us to the living room, where Bob sat down on the floor and I sat across the room on the sofa. When Bob placed Daisy on the floor, she ran over and jumped up on my lap. Astonished, the woman said, "I've never seen her do that." Still I was not convinced. I had a picture in my mind of what I wanted our dog to look like, and this was not it.

I suggested that since it was such a big decision, we would sleep on it and call in the morning. Once in the car, I began to question. Here I was holding out for a "pretty" dog, yet all of the pieces seemed to fall in line with the unusual way God might be bringing us our dog.

Within minutes of arriving home, we called the couple and told them we wanted to adopt Daisy. The next day, December 21, 2017, we picked up what we believed was our Christmas present from the Lord. We changed her name to Missy, and within a month or two, after her fur had grown out, I had my female, nonshedding, small to medium, fuzzy-wuzzy, doesn't smell like a dog, dog!

We took her down to meet Molly, and I did try to walk both dogs. But it didn't work out. Thankfully, Molly's momma had gained more strength and began walking Molly again.

Missy became my shadow. She spent time with Bob too, but generally she was with me. Where I went in the house, she went. Where I sat, she nestled close by. When I worked at my computer, she situated herself behind me on my chair, sometimes in the most uncomfortable-looking positions, just to be near me. If I stood at the kitchen sink to wash dishes, she was at my feet. She didn't want me out of her sight. One day, I looked down at her and asked, "Missy, are you that needy?" The question was barely out of my mouth when I thought, *Wait, maybe I'm the needy one. Maybe I'm Missy's assignment.*

Eighteen months to the day that we brought her home, a tragic accident took our Missy. When friends and family heard, we were inundated with condolences. I think, in fact, we received as many cards in the mail if not more than we received for our birthdays that year. With those comforting words, some who were dog owners suggested we begin looking for another dog to adopt.

About two weeks after I had cried about all the tears I could, I began taking quick peeks at the county shelter and humane society websites. Bob and I even made a few trips to both places. Then one Sunday afternoon as I perused the humane society website, there was Goldilocks, a two-year-old poodle mix who had been picked up as a stray. She certainly fit all of the items on my list, but what a mess. Her long, almost orange fur was matted in many places. Other parts of her were curly, thus the name Goldilocks.

I showed her photo to Bob. Both of us were emotionally weary from our two weeks of making visits to the county shelter and humane society only to be greeted by large barking dogs who looked like they could eat us on the spot. Bob said, "Look, you go see her. If you think she's the one, just text me. I can be there in minutes." I agreed and was first in line at the humane society before the doors opened on Monday morning.

The receptionist asked who I was there to see. "Goldilocks," I said. She then made an announcement over their intercom: "Bring Goldilocks to the meet and greet room. There's someone here to visit her."

I wasn't shocked at what the dog looked like, since I had already seen her website photo. Normally, shelter dogs are groomed before they are shown to anyone. For some reason, they decided to make Goldilocks adoptable in other ways before cleaning her up. The fella who brought her to me apologized for her appearance but assured me she was in good health, having spent the previous eight days in quarantine and having had all the necessary steps taken to ready her for adoption.

He then gave me toys and treats and left the two of us together. We played a bit. Then she allowed me to pick her up and hold her close. I had to look hard to find her eyes in all that overgrown fur, but when we did make eye contact, I just knew there was a treasure underneath all that hair, matting and all.

I took a selfie of Goldilocks and me and sent it to Bob, asking him to come. When Bob arrived, I watched their interaction. The two of them took to each other just as quickly as Goldilocks and I had, so I went back to the front desk to see about adoption. About thirty minutes later, once the paperwork was completed, the receptionist said over the intercom: "Bring Goldilocks up front. She's going home today." That morning, Bob and I walked out of the humane society, once again a family of three.

When we got home, we brought out everything we had accumulated for Missy: her crate, her washed and readied doggy beds and blankets, her few toys. It didn't take Goldilocks long to search out her new accommodations, going from one room to the other with one of us following close behind. She ravenously ate from her dish, gobbling up her food like it might be her last, probably from being a stray for who knows how long.

Immediately, we began thinking of names for our new fur baby. Somehow we just couldn't see ourselves calling out, "Goldilocks." Nothing came that first day, but when Bob came out of the shower the next morning, he said, "I think I have it! How about K-a-y-c-e-e, Kaycee?" I readily agreed.

We took Kaycee to be groomed that day. Believe me, the dog we took in was not the dog we brought out, at least in how she looked. We must have left half of her on the groomer's floor. Of course, we knew the groomer would have to take her down as close to her skin as possible. They said they hoped they would not find raw sores, which can happen with severely matted fur. Thankfully, they found nothing threatening, but now all we had was a tiny shaved dog with a huge bushy tail and full floppy ears. She was a sight, to be sure. Within a couple of months, her part-poodle fur grew out to reveal a beautiful, fuzzy-wuzzy, champagne-colored dog.

When we took her for her wellness check in that first seven days, Dr. Ed happily greeted us. "I'm so glad you didn't wait too long to get another dog," he said. "And rescue dogs are the best, you know. They are so appreciative." He then gave the three of us his blessing and Kaycee a clean bill of health.

As of this writing, we have had Kaycee a total of nine months, half the time we had our Missy girl. We are once again in love with our fur baby, who came to us on July 29, exactly five weeks to the day we lost Missy. I guess you could say that year we enjoyed a little Christmas in July.

From time to time, we mistakenly call her Missy, of course. But mostly, I call her "my girl" and Bob calls her "puppy." Besides his "puppy," she's Bob's playmate. Daily, almost like clockwork, Kaycee signals when it's playtime, and the two chase around the house. They even play hide and seek, Bob hiding and Kaycee doing the seeking.

Folks at church who mourned with us when we lost Missy kept close tabs on us and our progression in obtaining another dog. When we sent them photos of Kaycee, they were elated right along with us. One Sunday morning, one of them asked if we were spoiling her. "Oh yes," I readily replied. To which Bob asked, "Do you really think we're spoiling her?" To which I replied, referring to him, "How many dogs are walked around before bedtime and sung to?"

Who would have thought that as a result of a hurricane, we would be blessed with not one but two gifts in the form of two little bundles of fur that will forever have places in our hearts? For that, we are most grateful.

12

Born for This

Tracy Crump

When my husband, Stan, and I were newlyweds, warm summer evenings drew us from our high-rise apartment building onto the Memphis city streets. We wandered down tree-lined avenues past stately homes housing personalities such as opera star Marguerite Piazza. But it was on a smaller side street that we fell in love. Not with each other—we were already pretty settled on that—but with a gorgeous Siberian husky.

Whenever we came near his house, he perked up, triangular ears erect and a thick, luscious tail arched over his back in the husky stance. He strained the lead that staked him in the yard, trying to get to us, and we came as close as possible without encroaching on private property, all the while sweet-talking him. We made up our minds then. We would never have a mansion like those we admired, but one day . . .

A year and a half later, Stan and I became the proud owners of our first home—complete with a fenced-in backyard—and took possession in early December. What better time of the year to look for a new puppy? But how many breeders would have huskies, given our warm Southern climate? A quick perusal of the newspaper turned up one, and we called that evening for an appointment.

Six rambunctious teddy bears greeted us. I fell in love all over again. Since Stan wouldn't let me take all six home, I had to make a choice. Originally intent on getting a female, I learned the breeders were charging more for the solitary girl in the litter. Since the price already strained our budget, I turned my attention to the males. However, each one I picked up soon squirmed to get down and took off to tumble with his siblings. All except one.

When I picked up this one, he wrapped his front paws around my arm and looked into my face with one brown eye . . . and one blue. "Look at his eyes, Stan. How unusual. And he's so much calmer than the others. I like this one."

Stan reluctantly left a tug-of-war game with another puppy and came over to look. "That *is* odd. All right, we'll get him."

The owners told us later that having different-colored eyes wasn't an unusual trait in huskies, but by then, we were smitten. We took our new baby home and settled him in the bathroom for the night, complete with a blanket and stuffed animal to keep him company. Only he wasn't content. His whining and moaning kept us awake half the night. Not surprising for his first night away from his mother.

By the next morning, he'd developed a raspy cough, and I knew this was more than separation anxiety. I bundled him up, and we headed to the vet. When the doctor gave us the diagnosis, I couldn't believe it. Our Siberian husky—descended from a hardy line bred in one of the coldest regions of the world to pull sleds across miles of frozen wasteland—had a sinus infection.

Once our puppy recovered, his true personality emerged. He wasn't sedate at all but a bundle of energy. We gave him the impressive name of Nicholas Alexander, Niki for short, and began looking for ways to redirect our furry child's exuberance. He chewed the kitchen baseboards and ripped off wallpaper, so his days inside were numbered. As soon as we felt it safe, Stan built a doghouse and moved Niki into the yard. Thrilled to be outside, he would race around the perimeter so fast we couldn't keep up. He also loved to play soccer with Stan, capturing the ball between his front legs and dribbling it like a pro.

Niki made us proud when his innate intelligence shone during obedience school, and he won first place in his class. Still, we had to keep a constant eye on his destructive bent and had a hard time keeping him occupied and out of trouble.

Boredom wasn't our only enemy. Niki was born with the strong husky pack mentality, and his need for companionship sometimes resulted in retaliation when we didn't pay him enough attention. He once chewed our air-conditioner wiring; it's fortunate he didn't fry himself. When we went on vacation, he destroyed Stan's prized collection of bonsai, though he was smart enough to leave the cacti alone. If our household was going to survive, his intelligence and energy needed an outlet, a purpose.

As Niki matured, his beautiful black-and-white markings deepened, and silver highlights accented a luxurious coat. Other husky qualities emerged. With three-inch-long hair, he looked much larger than his forty-five pounds, and people often mistook him for a wolf. Those who ventured close enough said, "Oh, poor thing. He's blind," when they noticed his one ice-blue eye. Niki also didn't bark, another husky anomaly. However, he would howl when sirens sounded nearby.

Summers were understandably hard on Niki, who wore two coats—a dense, furry undercoat and a topcoat of longer hair. He spent most of the time lying in the shade and lapping bowlfuls of water until his thick undercoat began to loosen about midway through the season. Then we combed out, pulled out, and brushed out handfuls of fur until winter.

But oh, the winter! It was as if we watched hibernation in reverse. Though Memphis summers were brutally hot, our winters could still bite, and Niki became more and more active as temperatures plunged.

He came alive when the first snowflake fell. He jumped and nipped at the falling flakes and ran in frenzied circles to express his ecstasy. During his first winter, we got only a light dusting. But as Christmas approached the next year, several inches covered our backyard for days.

Then my husband had a brilliant idea.

Stan tracked down an old sled, a Christmas present from years past that had gone mostly unused since we had no downhill slope on which to ride. He hooked rope to it and made a harness of sorts. Niki eagerly put his head and legs into the traces, and off they went. Our "sled dog" pulled Stan, who weighed three to four times his weight, around the yard with ease. I could almost hear sleigh bells ringing and knew Santa would have been proud. It didn't even take eight reindeer to get the job done.

That simple sled ride was a turning point for our high-spirited canine. Harking back to the legendary huskies who rushed life-saving serum to Alaskan diphtheria victims in the early 1900s, Niki was happiest fulfilling a purpose. We all want to feel useful, and I guess dogs are no different. I once met a detective who said his bloodhound would die if he weren't allowed to track. Some dogs, through centuries of breeding, seem to be created for a particular purpose. Retrievers retrieve game. Shelties herd sheep. German shepherds protect their masters. Working dogs, which include huskies, are bred to assist us.

Whether acting as companions, guards, herders, or hunters, our canine friends know when we rely on them, and they shine brightest when meeting a need. Although we didn't *need* a sled dog, Niki seemed to see hauling Stan around as his mission, a joy rather than a burden.

After all, pulling a sled was what Niki was born to do.

13

A Dog Tail Christmas

Jenny Lynn Keller

My white Christmas story begins on the fourth of July when my husband and I went for a bicycle ride and returned with a puppy. We found him lying beside a fire hydrant in a new subdivision being developed. There were no houses in the area. How did he get there? Did he wander away from one of the nearby horse farms? Had someone not wanting a dog dropped him off? One thing for certain, he wouldn't survive long in the July heat without shade, food, and water, so we brought the white fluffy fur ball home.

After giving him a bath and removing a host of ticks and fleas, I discovered a thorn stuck in the middle of his tongue. Hungry and scared, the puppy accepted warm chicken broth but refused all attempts to extract the thorn. For the next two days, the poor little boy lapped on broth and mostly slept while we waited for the local veterinarian's office to reopen after the holiday weekend. During that time family and friends stopped by to see our newfound pup, and we began to call him Casey because his situation was such a sad *case* of circumstances—lost, starving, and hurt.

But that ball of white fluff shifted from sad to squirming when the veterinarian plucked the thorn from his tongue and declared him to be three months old based on the size of his sharp little teeth. She also warned us Casey would grow into a huge dog based on his paw size. Large, as in one-hundred-plus pounds, and tall, considering the length of his legs. Were we prepared to handle a dog that size if his owner never came forward? Uh, maybe.

The months rolled by, no one claimed Casey, and we welcomed a big addition to our household. I'm talking giant. Standing on his hind legs, the growing pup plopped his front paws on my shoulders every chance he got, and I'm taller than the average woman. Subsequent vet visits confirmed he was most likely the offspring of a Great Dane and Labrador retriever. We were the proud owners of a retriever fur and tail, Great Dane legs and chest, and the best combination of their personalities—friendly, easygoing, preferred the outdoors, and loved water. Right away Casey became the neighborhood children's favorite dog and our indoor cat's pesky younger brother. Years earlier, my Christmas-present kitten, Samantha, crowned herself Queen of Keller House and now refused all invitations to share her kingdom. No matter how hard Casey tried to convince her of his sincere desire to be friends, she rebuffed him with a hiss and swat on the nose.

But her rambunctious brother never tired of trying because we quickly learned he had two modes—off and on, mostly on. Casey lived to play and had the attention span of a gnat. Our two attempts at dog obedience school did show what a sweet, energetic, and gentle giant we had. But after one session, the first instructor kindly suggested we wait a few months and try again. The second class gave us more hope when we completed four sessions before being asked to leave. Casey's size and enthusiasm for everything and everyone distracted other students and enticed them to join him in fun. The promise of treats fell on preoccupied ears and eyes. Repeated practice of acceptable behavior like sit and stay resembled a comedy act. Casey's mind focused solely on adventure.

Which brings me to the Christmas portion of this story. I love everything about Christmas—the food, decorations, get-togethers, spirit of giving, and most of all the real reason for the season. To celebrate our first Christmas in a house with tall ceilings, I bought a twelve-foot tree for our living room and looked forward to decorating it. While my husband and pets watched television with their eyes mostly closed the first weekend in December, I strung hundreds of miniature white lights, hung a variety of ornaments, and draped yards of garland on the tree. A flip of the light switch sold me on the finished product, so I continued filling the other rooms with greenery, holly berry sprigs, and candles. We planned to host several parties of family and friends over the next few weeks, and I wanted our house to look and smell like Christmas.

On Monday, my husband and I went to work and returned to a house filled with Christmas decorations not where I had originally placed them. Had we been ransacked and robbed by someone who hated Christmas? A thorough check revealed no missing valuables and all doors and windows locked. What in the world happened to our house? Another glance at the Christmas tree provided a clue. While it remained upright and in place, the bottom half contained no ornaments. Okay, who in this house could remove nearly six feet of red satin Christmas balls and scatter them to every room? Hmm, let me guess. His back stood three feet off the floor, his bushy tail wagged another two feet higher, and his long snout had a reputation for going where it had no business. But I'd never seen Casey bat around small objects the size of a softball. Did he have a feline partner in crime?

That night I redecorated the lower half of the Christmas tree, and the next evening we returned home to the same situation.

No doubt major partying occurred in our absence, and I was determined to discover who was doing what. How could such mayhem occur when both pets settled in their favorite sleeping places after breakfast each morning and we found them in the same location hours later? Were we being hoodwinked by our two furry children?

The third day we came home early, parked several houses away, and sneaked a peek through the living room windows. In broad daylight we caught the rascals in joyous mischief. Casey pranced around the Christmas tree, swishing his tail against the branches and knocking off ornaments. Samantha pounced on the satin balls, batted them left and right across the large room, and chased escapees down the hallway. We couldn't help but laugh as we witnessed a brother-and-sister tag-team wrestling match against our Christmas tree. Casey had found favor with the Queen of Keller House, and our poor tree was paying the price.

What should we do? The satin balls now resembled semi-peeled Red Delicious apples. Drastic measures might be necessary, and it wouldn't be the first time we'd implemented them in the last six months. You see, we lived in a subdivision with a golf course meandering through it, and our house sat along the seventh fairway. To Casey's delight, most golfers' first stroke off the seventh tee landed within easy running distance of our backyard. The Labrador retriever part of him couldn't resist recovering golf balls falling out of the sky, bouncing on the ground, and rolling across the manicured greenway. His ancestors had been trained to retrieve waterfowl, and he couldn't let them down. But the golfers responded with less enthusiasm, especially when Casey dented or cracked their golf balls with his teeth. To keep the peace and our neighbors happy, we installed an underground electric pet fence. Oh, the things parents do to protect their children.

But how could I protect my Christmas tree? Confining Casey to a room or the garage always resulted in more mischief. One of our bathrooms sported the scars—shredded wallpaper, scratched door, chewed drapes, and tattered rug. This Christmas our pets made Santa's naughty list, and one of them had the potential of becoming a permanent resident. With our first party only days away, I made a parental decision and decided sometimes less is best. The bottom half of the Christmas tree sparkled with lights but no ornaments.

Over the next few weeks, family and friends came to visit, commented on our half-naked tree, and heard our dog tail story. They laughed and rewarded the culprit with a pat or belly rub, and our fluffy white fur ball soaked up the attention. He also learned a new skill. With all the holiday company and food, our gentle giant discovered his head was tall enough to rest on the dining room table and his tongue could reach any dish within a foot of the edge. This new game topped the Christmas tree swish for the rest of his life because the reward was food.

My biggest lesson from our first Christmas with Casey was just as rewarding. I learned fun is more satisfying than perfection when it comes to pets, Christmas decorations, and other things in life. A truth I repeated to myself and others many times over the next thirteen years with Casey. Oh, the tales I could tell you about that fluffy white dog tail.

14

The Dog Who Came to Christmas

Denise Fleck

Pooches was a lab, terrier, Heinz 57 mix who ruled the ridge in the Hollywood Hills where my husband and I shared our first home. A welterweight in the retriever category, she stood taller than her height and was wise beyond her years. She belonged to the couple at the apex of the hill, and although they loved her and looked after her, Pooches considered us her second family. She was an outdoor dog who I think somehow longed for the cushier comforts of home. I'd often let her into our fence when we were doing yard work, and on rainy California nights, we would sneak her in our front door, where she stayed in the entry, seemingly grateful for the shelter. If I ever had any doubt (honestly, I didn't), she was the dog who confirmed my suspicion that humans are not the only life-form to possess emotion.

Pooches was a constant companion to our own yellow Labrador, Sunny. One chilly morning, Sunny woke up in pain, unable to move. For the most easygoing of labs who never complained about anything, every movement seemed to cause Sunny great pain. We lived several hundred feet uphill from our car, so we had a vet tech come to our house. This situation would end happily, but we didn't know that yet.

I will never forget the concern exhibited by our doggie friend, Pooches. It was as touching a moment as I have ever experienced. Pooches wandered into our yard through the open gate and, with such a look of concern in her graying face, licked Sunny's cheek. She then nudged Sunny's ear several times with her nose and whimpered a gentle sigh. As we lifted the stretcher, the small black dog stood back to clear the way and then let out a sharp and forceful bark addressed toward Sunny as if to say, "Don't worry, pal. You'll be all right, and I'll keep watch until you get back." Pooches paced self-confidently back and forth at the top of the hillside as we carried the ailing Sunny-dog down the long and winding steps. I'm happy to report that Sunny recovered and enjoyed many more fun adventures.

Pooches continued to stop by each morning, during the afternoon, and at dusk, politely asking for a cookie. On occasion she'd bring another neighborhood dog to our front door as well, and before long, those other dogs would appear on their own, barking polite requests for treats. Poochie, as I sometimes called her, however, remained special, and when her family went out of town, I had the pleasure of feeding her.

One such time, on Christmas Eve, my husband, Paul, and I bid our Sunny adieu and headed on foot to a neighbor's holiday party. Like she so often did, Pooches was snoozing on our doorstep, and when we stepped out, she eagerly wagged, hoping for a cookie and a pat on the head. It was a drizzly evening, and darkness had come early. Even though it was Southern California, the wetness made the night chilly, so we hoped that Pooches would head to her comfy doghouse up on the ridge.

Pooches had other plans.

Umbrella in hand, we made our way down the hillside on 110 railroad-tie steps to the street below. Pooches began to follow us. Hearing her footsteps behind us, we gently shooed her home several times, but we'd look back, and there she was again. Pooches spent her whole life patrolling the ridge and knew it well, but we were venturing down into the more densely packed housing area, and we wanted her to stay safe and dry. We coaxed her back up the hill and continued down the narrow winding street as the rain poured down.

When we arrived at the door with host gifts in hand, I felt a nuzzle at my right calf. Pooches! The neighbor knew we had a yellow dog, and this was a smaller black canine with a graying face. I introduced Pooches and said I'd quickly return her back to her home. I walked her home, then walked back to our host's home. My husband and I settled in with the others, consuming delicacies and sharing in conversation. Then another guest arrived to partake in the festivities, and on his heels, a very wet Pooches appeared! "Where did this wet mess of a dog come from?" someone inquired.

Embarrassed, I explained that she must have followed us, and our host kindly said, "No worries! Let me get a towel and dry her off." Hearing my voice, Pooches beelined toward me, and fortunately, I grabbed the towel from our host and placed it on her just as she was about to give a giant doggie shake. Once dried, the little dog settled to my side, smack-dab in front of the roaring fireplace, curled into a ball, and fell fast asleep. Every once in a while, an ear would prick up at cacophonous laughter or as the scent of a new hors d'oeuvres tray drifted past.

In spite of the slight scent of wet dog, everyone was amazed at how this small outdoor pooch, a little rough around the collar, settled in so politely and quietly. Whether she thought her place was by my side as protector or whether she wanted to experience some creature comforts, she thrilled the host and guests alike, and she became the topic of conversation. By the time gifts were exchanged, Pooches had recharged from her nap, and she sat up attentively. Being the goofy dog mom that I am, I had baked cookies for the neighbors' own pets, and each of them kindly snuck one from their package for Pooches (not knowing she had her own gift bag at our house). As wrappings were undone, a shiny red ribbon fell to the floor, and the host (not a pet parent himself) reached down and tied it to Pooches's collar. You would have thought she was a princess receiving her first tiara as she properly lowered her head and allowed access to her neck. Pooches *pawsitively* glowed!

As the evening wound down and the rain stopped, guests began to depart, each one petting Pooches good night and wishing all a merry Christmas. The sweet little dog who came to Christmas followed us back up the hill and slept in our entryway—on a warm blanket, of course—with visions of dog cookies dancing in her head.

The very next Christmas, I am pleased to say that not only were we still enjoying daily visits from our pal Pooches, but the neighbor who had hosted the previous year's party adopted his first-ever dog. And doggone it—it was a Pooches look-alike!

15

Our Lucky Christmas

Lauraine Snelling

O ur first house. Not a rental, but ours. All five of us stood in the front doorway and stared inside.

"Looks big, doesn't it?" I glanced up at Wayne to catch his nod.

"Wait till we fill it with furniture."

"And a dog." Kevin, our oldest son at six, stared up at his dad. Ever since our snow-white Samoyed started chasing sheep that did not belong to us, we had been dog-less. As far as Wayne was concerned, we were in no hurry to get another dog.

We walked through the brand-new house, my mind clicking into list mode. Curtains—I planned to sew them all—curtain rods, towel rods. While the house was carpeted throughout in dark green, I needed color. Every house in the development had a garage and the same small purple-leafed trees in the front yard. No fences at ours or the houses around us. I intensely dislike fences, but in town like this they would be a necessity. Probably project number one.

"A dog sure will have lots to see and smell out here," Kevin observed.

The Green River bordered the development, so we had a nice little river less than a block away. Kevin and Wayne could almost go fishing from our yard.

"We can go swimming in the river and take our dog." Five-year-old Marie would have preferred a horse, but that would not happen in this small space.

Fifteen feet from one house wall to the next. At least the back-yard was big enough for a reasonable garden.

Over the next couple of weeks, we got moved and settled in. Sheets were tacked to cover the windows at night, but we had a house. It even had a fireplace.

"Hey, Mom," Marie said one day, "we can hang our stockings on the fireplace for Christmas. We can hang one up for Chai Lai too." Our Siamese cat had been given to us as a wedding present.

"Sure 'nough." That meant we needed a mantel first. I added it to the list.

I turned to answer our also green telephone hanging on the wall in the kitchen right by the back door.

"Hello, this is your brother calling."

I was shocked to say the least. He rarely called and never during the day. "Well, hello to you too. Is everything all right?"

"Oh yah, but . . ."

I waited.

"I have a big favor to ask."

"Okay." He never asked for favors. In fact, we hardly ever talked.

"You know my dog, Lucky?"

"Yes."

"I-I need to find a home for Lucky, and I'm sure hoping you can take her. She is so great with kids; about the best dog I've ever known."

"But why are you giving her away?"

He paused and cleared his throat. "I just need to. We've moving into town, and I can't take her with me." Don and his wife had been living on our mother's farm after our father passed away.

"But . . ." My mind was spinning faster than a windmill with why's and what's and . . .

"Just, please, will you take her?"

I could hear tears in his voice. He loved that dog so much. "I have to ask Wayne."

"I know but . . ."

"I'll call you back as soon as he gets home from work."

"If you can come get her this weekend . . ."

Now I was sniffing and blinking. "Sure." I turned to see all three kids staring at me.

"We're getting a dog. Lucky."

Kevin, mouth open, kept staring at me.

"We still have to ask Dad."

All three nodded, eyes dancing.

"She's a big dog." Brian at three, almost four, as he kept telling everyone, leaned up against me.

"Uncle Don says she's the best dog ever. She likes to lick." Marie wiggled. Standing still was not part of her makeup. "Lucky really likes to play."

The three met Wayne when he parked his pickup on the slanted slab into the garage. So much for my gently telling him the situation.

We left early Saturday morning to drive from Auburn, Washington, to the farm in Silverdale, Washington, about a two-hour drive.

After a day spent playing with the calves down at the creek, the kids and Lucky came back up muddy. Then they were out in the fields, throwing sticks for Lucky. Eventually we loaded back in the car with a leash and collar. Don gave us strict instructions on how to make sure the dog kept up her training. She was to sit on the floor in the car, sleep in the garage, never eat people food nor beg at the table, never get up on the furniture. When she was in the house, she should stay on her rug. Wayne needed to build a pen for her.

We waved goodbye, the proud owners of a seventy-pound, red-coated, German shorthaired/lab cross dog. I heard her whimper from the back seat where she sat on the floor. I knew she'd miss my brother, but he'd miss her even more. Sometimes life just wasn't fair.

When it got quiet in the back seat, I turned to see all three kids sound asleep, Marie and Kevin using Lucky for a pillow and Brian curled up on his blankie on the floor. Lucky thumped her tail and looked guilty.

Needless to say, after Lucky whined and finally barked from the garage the first night, she never slept there again, and it didn't take her long to decide that the foot of the lower bunk where Kevin slept was her place. She loved to ride in the truck with Wayne, sitting up right next to him; bench seats were in vogue back then. The back seat of the car was fine as long as the window was rolled partway down and she had her kids around her.

Even she and the cat became friends after a few lessons in the house rules from Chai Lai. I was surprised at that, although Don had said Lucky got along with the cats at the farm. Lucky got along with everyone unless they approached the house, car, or truck without our invitation. No one ever argued with her. Her bark made her sound fierce, but the only dangerous part of her was her wagging tail, which had been known to leave bruises and clear off the coffee table.

One day Marie asked, "Mom, how are we going to hang our Christmas stockings above the fireplace? It's all brick."

"Good question. We better get that mantel up." I had an idea what I wanted but that was as far as it had gone. The next day I was at a lumberyard searching for the perfect piece of wood. God sure blessed me that day as I left with a four-by-four hunk of mahogany and no idea how Wayne would turn that into a mantel. But I handled the sanding and finishing, and he and a neighbor wrestled it into place.

The kids and I were in awe. And it wasn't even December yet. That definitely was a miracle.

Like always, December arrived like a freight train without a whistle. Since I always made Christmas presents, the sewing machine hummed, and as usual some people received a card with a note saying their present would be ready before the new year.

That year when we went Christmas shopping, mostly to look at the decorations, we swung by a pet store for a new collar and three toys for Lucky, one from each of the kids. They even shut Lucky out of the room as they wrapped her presents.

Lucky and Chai Lai both watched as we put up the first Christmas tree in our new home. We placed it in the dining room because we didn't have a table and chairs there yet—right in front of the window. We had it all set up when the cat jumped up on the windowsill to inspect the tree, and Lucky tried to crawl under it to discover whatever she could sniff. The tree rocked, the cat leaped to safety, and Lucky backpedaled as fast as she could with the tree crashing around her. At least we had not decorated it yet. Wayne was not a happy camper.

To keep this from happening again, we strung wires to hooks into the window frame, but we needn't have bothered. Neither dog nor cat wanted anything more to do with that green monster. After we decorated the tree, we hung the empty stockings from the mantel.

"Lucky, see, you have a stocking too." Kevin showed her but she looked at him with a shrug and lay down in front of the fireplace.

"I don't think she's too impressed." I looked up at Wayne, who was shaking his head. He sat down on the sofa, and Lucky leaped up to snuggle next to him. "Good thing Don hasn't seen how we've spoiled his dog."

"She's our dog now, that's for sure." He got a quick ear lick for hugging her.

We always attended the candlelight service on Christmas Eve, one of my favorite services of the year. As usual, Brian fell asleep on my lap, Marie leaned against her dad on one side and Kevin on the other. No one argued about going to bed that night. They all staggered into the house and stayed awake just long enough to get into their jammies and crawl into bed. Lucky took her place with Kevin.

Wayne finished putting a trike together while I located all the presents to stack under the tree and filled the stockings.

"The stockings are too heavy to hang back up."

Wayne shook his head. "Lay 'em on the hearth." And he shuffled down the hall to our bedroom. Putting the trike together had destroyed any Christmas cheer he had left.

"Sure, and the dog and cat will get in them." I laid the stockings on the kitchen table and followed him. Chai Lai was curled in her usual place at the foot of our bed.

Far sooner than we'd hoped, we woke to three giggling kids scrambling up on our bed.

"Mom, Dad, Christmas is here!"

"Are you sure?" I asked, trying to blink my eyes open. "You didn't go out in the living room yet . . ."

"No, you said . . ."

"I know." I grabbed my robe. "Maybe we should have breakfast first."

"M-o-m!" Three voices in absolute unison. "Hurry."

"I am. I am. Get your dad up too." I could hear them begging him to get moving. I plugged in the tree lights, laid the stuffed stockings out on the hearth, and announced all was ready. Down the hall they charged, kids, dog, cat, and Dad somewhere behind them.

"Oh, it's so pretty." Marie looked up at me, her eyes shining. We all stood quietly for a moment.

"Can we open our presents now?"

"How about stockings first while I make coffee and hot chocolate?"

They each found their stocking and handed the animals theirs. Sniffing commenced.

We had our hot drinks and devoured the plate of julekake, Norwegian Christmas bread, and some cookies while the children showed us what was in their stockings. Lucky lay on the floor beside us, working on the bone that had been in her stocking. Chai Lai batted at a catnip-stuffed felt mouse.

Kevin held up Lucky's stocking. "We never had a dog stocking before."

"We never had a dog like Lucky before either." Wayne reached over and ruffled Lucky's ears. Her tail thumped on the carpet as she kept on gnawing on her bone.

I wasn't sure who was most blessed, us or the dog. But watching Marie give her a present to unwrap and offering to help her made my grin even wider, both inside and out. Maybe we'd be referring to this through the coming years as the Lucky Christmas.

16

A Makeover for Cindy

Claudia Wolfe St. Clair

Some Christmases stand out more than others when skipping down memory lane. The one I revisit time and again is the year there were two visitors at Christmastime, one a human, one a dog.

My best friend Donna was coming from Seattle for the first time since I'd moved to Toledo. The guest room was decked out for Christmas. Everything was ready for her arrival.

It was also the year my oldest, Dawn, was traveling from Denver with plans to visit me, then take a longer road trip east to visit more family. Accompanying her was Cindy, a large gray terrier mix.

Cindy had been abandoned in Spring Lake, North Carolina. When Dawn was assigned to Fort Bragg, she was cleared to live off post. While checking out apartments, she came across a friendly stray dog. The folks at the rental office had been feeding her and trying to find her a home. The dog followed Dawn around the complex with hopeful eyes as she looked at several places.

The rental agent, bent on matchmaking, offered lower rent if Dawn would take the dog. Dawn agreed. She found a place she could call home and a companion to share it. Thus began a mutually beneficial partnership. She named the dog Cindy.

Cindy became the constant in Dawn's life through two more moves. She adjusted with ease to new locations as long as she had Dawn.

Not all the points on Dawn's upcoming road trip were dog friendly. Without hesitation, I offered to keep Cindy during the holidays. Easy-peasy.

"She's going to expect to sleep with you."

"Well, she's going to be disappointed."

When she realized she was alone with me, Cindy spent a lot of time facing the door, waiting. *Surely she's coming back.* After a lot of coaxing and sweet talk, Cindy and I settled into a routine of daily walks ending with games of fetch at the arboretum down the street. She spent a little less time watching the door. She was good company.

When Donna arrived, the energy level of the household rose significantly. We had so much catching up to do! She was just as excited to share her visit with Cindy. Donna was more than willing to lavish attention on Cindy, taking her for extra playtime at the park. It was great.

Between us we agreed to give Cindy a makeover. We'd start by giving her a haircut. Cindy did not share our enthusiasm for this idea. The only way forward was for one of us to distract her while the other snipped carefully. We would stop when Cindy had enough of our nonsense. Grooming sessions were brief. The haircut took several days.

A quick trip to a pet store netted a good brush and lavender-scented doggie shampoo. The haircut experience was a stretch for Cindy to endure. A bath was the final straw. Thank heaven there were two of us to tag-team Cindy into an empty tub. The bathroom door was closed to prevent escape.

Donna held on to her and spoke gently while water was added to the tub. We talked and soothed her as the indignity of her bath progressed. Lather, rinse, repeat. We drained the water and lifted a heavy, dripping dog to a waiting stack of old towels. Together we towel-dried her and graduated to a blow dryer. Obviously, she was not happy about that. But a chorus of "Good girl! Look how pretty you look!" seemed to do the trick. What could she do? She was trapped in a bathroom between two soaking-wet women.

After everything she had been through, she allowed us to brush her. All fluffy and fragrant, she looked like a different dog.

Every December I host a holiday gathering at my house, and it was just a few days away. We shifted into all-out party preparation with all of the tension that entails. Cindy followed us everywhere and made sure we took frequent breaks to play at the arboretum. Her presence kept us grounded.

The night of the party, Cindy greeted every guest at the door. She was her friendly self. No barking, and even more impressive, she didn't steal anyone's food. She was perfect.

Donna's visit was marked with long talks on the couch with Cindy between us. We discussed our hopes and plans for the future in detail. We shared the dog's brush and groomed Cindy within an inch of her life. Dawn would be greeted by a four-legged glamour girl in a few days.

Donna's departure date came too soon. She left early on Christmas Eve for the next phase of her Christmas visits. We'd had a wonderful time filled with laughter, tears, and the company of my "grandpuppy."

Cindy and I had a quiet Christmas, just the two of us. It was clear and cold, no snow. We took longer walks around the neighborhood, enjoying companionable silence. The air smelled of woodsmoke from many fireplaces along the way.

We had the arboretum to ourselves. Cindy's favorite game of fetch with her tennis ball was good exercise for us both. She didn't notice the squirrels when the ball was in play. Only the cold would send us back indoors.

The day passed with family phone calls and old Christmas movies from the forties on television. Cindy was by my side.

Knowing she would soon be on her way back to Denver, I had a sudden need to rethink my position on sleeping arrangements. Getting ready for bed after a peace-filled Christmas day, I patted the bed beside me.

"Come on up, girl." She did. No need for her to be disappointed anymore.

17

An Unforgettable Christmas Surprise

Jane Owen

On a sunny December afternoon in 1968, I remarked to my new husband, "It's hard to believe it's almost Christmas, Ron." I gazed out our small kitchen window. "Without snow, it doesn't feel too Christmassy."

He raised his eyebrows. "Snowy weather would be a miracle here in Florida."

During our first year as newlyweds, we moved to Pensacola to lead a student campus ministry. We were eager to settle in to Florida's sandy beaches, warm sea breezes, and beautiful palm trees.

Now I watched as palm fronds swayed in our yard. "Back home in Ohio there are several feet of snow, according to the latest report." I gave Ron a playful look. "It's for sure you won't miss shoveling that white stuff!"

He nodded. "You wouldn't be wrong." He took a deep breath. "Why don't we take a sightseeing drive around Pensacola?"

"Yes, let's! I'd like a tour around town."

The drive was relaxing until Ron turned off onto an unmarked road.

"Why did you turn onto this dirt lane?" I saw a dilapidated house at the end of the narrow path. I put my hand on Ron's arm. "You are going to turn around, aren't you?"

Ron smiled and pulled the car next to the shabby house. "We have an appointment to pick out your Christmas present."

"What? Here?"

"Come on, Jane. Don't mind the looks of the place. I agree it's a little rough. But I saw an ad in the newspaper and talked to the owner to arrange our visit." He stepped around to my side and opened the door. For a fleeting second, I thought I detected hesitancy in him as he eyed the broken walk to the porch stoop and chickens clucking about the yard.

"It will be fine," he assured. "I asked the Lord to show me how to surprise you this Christmas." He gave me a wry grin. "I believe this is it."

He took my arm and escorted me around several ruts up to the weathered door. The door opened, and a grandmotherly woman welcomed us.

"Hello. You must be the Owenses. I'm Greta. Come in."

I followed Ron inside, noting the tidiness of the entry room. *Thankfully, this doesn't match the outside.* Then I heard whimpering. "Do I hear puppies?"

"Yes, you do," Greta answered. "Four peekapoo pups are left from the litter of seven."

"Peekapoo?"

"Yes. These puppies are a mix of Pekingese and poodle. Daddy was a Pekingese. Momma was a toy poodle. They are an exceptional breed! Simply irresistible!" she gushed.

Hmm, a practiced sales pitch. I smiled politely.

Greta led us into a small room where balls of tumbling fur greeted us.

"Oh, Ron! How cute!" I exclaimed, taking small steps around bustling paws.

Greta gave me a knowing look. "This blended breed is both intelligent and affectionate. I will put them together in this open crate so you can choose the one you want."

I looked at Ron. "I don't know which one . . ."

"Take your time," he said.

I squeezed his hand. "Let's decide together. I want him to be our Christmas pup."

Greta excused herself, saying, "It's almost dinnertime for them. I'll only be a minute."

While the puppies continued their playful jostling in the crate, one pulled up on the side and cried after Greta. I reached past it to pick up the smallest of the litter.

"What about you, cutie?" It trembled and pulled away.

Ron's attention focused on the whining black-and-tan puppy. "How about this one?" He stroked the little noisemaker's head.

I lifted him out of the crate. He wagged his tail and licked my hand. He nestled in my arms like he belonged, and my heart knew. "Yes, let's get him!"

Greta returned with a large food bowl and grinned. "Have you chosen that friendly guy?"

"We have," Ron answered. "May we come back to get him in a couple of days?"

"Certainly! You'll need time to gather doggie things before you take him home."

"Thank you, Greta. May I hold him a little longer?"

"Of course! He's yours!" When he squirmed, I put him down to eat and watched him nudge himself in between the others.

Greta leaned toward Ron, lowering her voice, "You may pay the thirty dollars when you return to pick him up."

Back at the car, Ron opened the door for me. "I overheard Greta," I said. "Can we afford thirty dollars on our budget?"

"I'm sorry you heard her—sort of spoiled my surprise. No problem, though. I've been saving some bucks here and there, hoping to keep it a secret."

"You sweetheart!" I threw my arms around him. "Thank you for such a darling Christmas surprise!"

That evening we brainstormed names for our peekapoo boy. Nothing gelled until I recalled the name meaning *promise*. "Let's name him Homer!"

Ron's smile reflected in his blue eyes. "Why not? I like the thought of him as a promise."

"Homer needs a middle name too," I added. "How about Alexander?"

"What does that mean?"

"I don't know. But it's a strong name, and Homer Alexander sounds just right to me."

We decided not to wait two days to pick up our peekapoo. Early the next morning, we arrived at Greta's.

"You've picked a winner!" she said, putting our puppy in my arms. "What's his name?"

"Homer Alexander." I scratched him behind his ears.

"That's an impressive name. I bet you'll love living life with your Homer Alexander."

Her words proved truthful beyond what we imagined.

That first day, we allowed Homer to explore our small trailer home. He sniffed around corners and under the bed. We sat on the couch, enjoying his every move. Suddenly he made a running leap into our laps.

"You've made yourself at home, haven't you, boy?" Ron said. "Let's go outside and let you run around."

Homer inspected every inch of our fenced yard. When he finished his outdoor inspection, he sat down at our feet and yipped. Cocking his head, he wagged his tail that curled over his back.

"He wants to go inside." I started up the steps with Homer on my heels.

"I didn't know you were a peekapoo interpreter," Ron commented with a wide grin.

After a long drink of water, Homer hopped up on the couch, stretching out across our laps. "You're a contented wonder," I said, enjoying the warmth of his furry closeness.

At bedtime, we put him in a temporary cardboard crate down the hall from our bedroom. I rubbed him under the chin. "This is your sleeping spot for now, Homer. See you in the morning."

Off to bed we went, but Homer commenced crying, followed by sharp yips.

"We may have to do something different, Jane. He's not settling down, and if he starts to howl . . ."

"Give him time. It's his first night."

With that, Ron wrapped his pillow around his head.

After a little while, Homer quieted down. We slept peacefully. The next morning, all was quiet. Too quiet. I stepped out of bed and discovered our sleeping pup, curled up on my slippers beside our bed.

"Ron," I whispered, "look who's still sleeping." We giggled, and Homer's ears twitched. He awoke, greeting us with licks and leaps.

"How did you get out of your crate, little boy?"

"Come here, Jane. You'll see."

The crate lay on its side. I scooped Homer up. "You are one clever fellow. You hung on the side of this flimsy structure, tipped it over, and scampered out, didn't you?" He answered with a quick lick across my face. That day we purchased a dog bed and placed it in a corner of our bedroom.

Adventures with Homer continued. One evening he went outside to do his business. We heard growls and serious snarls. "Ron, something's after Homer!"

I flung the door open. Homer stood at the bottom of the steps with a huge pine cone in his mouth. "Get the camera, Ron!"

He snapped the first shot. The second one caught Homer ready to come inside, gripping the prickly prey in his teeth. As he pranced back to his bed to deposit his prize, Ron clicked the third picture.

Homer studied us as we dissolved in belly laughs. The "critter" must have poked him that night because we found it laying at the front door the next morning.

Another episode occurred some weeks later. Our fenced yard had two gates. One gate pulled and the other gate pushed to open.

Our neighbors nearest us in the trailer park invited us for lunch. We left Homer to play in our yard. I peeked out their door several times, checking on our Mr. Curious. At one point, I spied him exploring the closest gate to our friends' home.

"Don't worry, Jane," said Ron. "Homer is safely enclosed. He'd have to pull that gate to escape."

Minutes later, Homer barked at our friends' door. I observed the open gate and picked him up. "You're a Houdini hound," I declared.

Ron shook his finger in Homer's face. "How did you figure out how to pull that gate?"

I hugged our little dog. "You are one persistent pup, Homer Alexander."

Our friend Nancy ran her fingers through his silky fur. "Persistent in love for the two of you, I'd say."

Homer was a year old when Ron and I took him on a walk one evening. "We don't want night to catch us, Jane. Let's turn around in this cul-de-sac."

Before we turned fully toward home, a full-grown German shepherd rushed out at us. The fur bristled the length of its back. Ferocious growls sounded his intent. I froze, realizing Homer was the target. The huge dog lunged. In that instant, Homer stood upright on his back legs. Huddling up under the shepherd's massive head, he thrust his paws around its neck.

Abruptly, that shepherd's threatening demeanor changed. It literally turned tail and ran back to its porch. Our frisky warrior led the way home with jaunty steps.

"Do you believe it, Ron? That dog looked like a Goliath, but Homer didn't flinch. He put himself between us and that vicious attacker and hugged the meanness right out of him!"

Ron reached down and patted Homer. "Boy, that brave maneuver sure showed your bold defensive instincts."

A few years later, Ron and I relocated to Ohio. We bought our first home on a tree-lined country road. Ron took a job in Columbus, and I signed a contract to teach first grade in a nearby town.

One afternoon, I said, "Our work schedules mean that Homer will spend long days alone. What can we do?"

Ron shook his head. "I've thought about this too. He needs companionship. Leaving him alone for hours each day troubles me."

"And we can't bear to be separated from him either."

"What about your friend Lila and her three boys? Think about how Homer enjoyed playing with them when we visited last summer."

"Yes, and remember what Lila said?"

Ron remained quiet for a bit. "I do. Lila offered to take him if we ever needed to make a change."

Tears spilled down my cheeks as I stroked our faithful pet, tucked between us on the couch. "Maybe that family is Homer's answer."

The next week, we took Homer to his new home. Lila's boys disappeared with him into their backyard. Homer's delight showed as he ran, jumping after the boys, retrieving the ball they threw for him. I watched from her backdoor window, struggling to convince myself this situation was best for our frolicking bundle of energy.

Ron stood behind me and spoke quietly. "We need to be going." With a hurried goodbye, we slipped out Lila's front door and drove home in silence.

That following week, we kept reassuring ourselves that our beloved Homer was happy and content with his new family. But our hearts yearned for him.

Finally, I couldn't resist. "Do you think he's all right? I could call and check on him."

Ron handed me the phone. I quickly dialed Lila's number.

She answered and said, "I was about to call you, Jane. Homer sat up at the front door the day you left. He didn't move until the boys took him back out to play. While they are at school, he returns to the door and stares out the screen." She paused. "He's waiting for you."

We didn't waste a second getting to her house. There he was, sitting up at the screen door. Spying us, Homer nosed it open. In a flash, he tore out and leaped into my arms. What a tearful reunion, complete with a face-bath for Ron and me.

The most heartwarming example of Homer's sensitive nature happened when my father, suffering in the last stages of cancer, came to spend a few days with us in our country home.

That first morning, we didn't find Homer in his bed. We wondered, but not long. When my dad came down the hall from his room, I said, "Someone is trailing you."

"Yes," he replied, "he kept me company last night."

"Were you able to sleep?" Ron asked.

My dad chuckled as he bent over to pet Homer. "I enjoyed a great night of rest with my unexpected companion!"

"Did he disturb you, Dad?"

"Not at all. Most nights, I can't sleep. The pain meds don't hold me. But your compassionate pooch snuggled in next to me and comforted me through the night."

As we ate breakfast, Homer stayed by Dad's chair. Whenever Dad looked at Homer, our begging pup sat up, hoping to get a bite of bacon. "You're hard to resist, my friend," Dad said, dispensing the treat.

"Now, Dad," I gently protested, treasuring the moment.

Each night of Dad's visit, Homer shadowed him. Even for afternoon naps in the recliner, Homer crawled right up beside him. On the last day, he remarked, "Your Homer was good medicine for me. I'll miss him."

"He's going to miss you too, Dad." I hugged him. "Visit again soon, and we know Homer will gladly give you more doses of his medicine."

My 1968 Christmas surprise surely was a canine character, delivering joy on steroids. Moreover, his personality defined unconditional love and loyalty. Still today, Homer Alexander remains in our hearts as the promise that came true.

18

Luke's Reindeer Games

DJ Perry

Our Luke might have been named for the biblical follower of Jesus or maybe the cool-handed Western gunslinger or just maybe the intergalactic hero adventuring in a galaxy far, far away. Luke was our rescued pit bull, who we adopted despite my initial concerns about bringing my first non-Labrador and male dog into our family. He was the last puppy left from a litter when we went to meet him. I admit that he had me a touch cautious, but from the first time this proud puppy confidently strutted into the room looking like a walking cup of hazelnut coffee, I was in love.

It was our guess that this handsome pup might see fifty or sixty pounds of weight, but soon he passed those projected benchmarks and kept growing. He grew strong, looking like ninety pounds plus of young lion, and he was admired by everyone. Admired even more for his relaxed attitude and natural charm that brought him a "good citizenship award" and the love of most all who knew him, especially the ladies.

Luke loved all the stops on the seasonal wheel, but to him winter always seemed the most magical. Luke's furry sister Joplin taught him to love the first falling snowflakes that fly as the season begins. The run-up to Christmas was also a favorite since that time was always shared with many friends and family. Luke also loved to open presents. His excitement was on the level of a three-year-old gift-drunk child waging a berserker battle against wrapping paper, string, and tape. Although he shared the house with several other furry siblings, he would nonetheless always go to *his* stocking, almost as if he could read his own name. He just loved, like many of our dogs, to nibble, nudge, and attack the shiny wrapping paper to reveal the mystery within—maybe a nylon bone, a Kong, or an assortment of treats.

Even in the snow, Luke loved to walk and explore nature and did so often because he was so good with people. But to explore in winter means to be prepared, and this goes for humans and dogs alike. In the short days when Jack Frost danced about powdering the state of Michigan, our short-haired buddy embraced his momma's selection of doggie shirts, jackets, and sweaters. Our boy did not possess the furry yeti feet of our female lab, Daphne. Her Einstein-like hair growing between her toes was reminiscent of the ears and eyebrows of a few past science professors. We tried the doggie boots that might work fine with a dainty dog, but with large Luke, they lasted under a minute before joining a plethora of closeted items bought and never used again.

One of the grand adventures that Luke enjoyed most was the trip to the local Christmas tree farm. First you have to understand that dogs love a car ride, and Luke was no exception. Much like "Where's your momma?", "Who wants to get grandma?", and "Who wants to go for a walk?", the phrase, "Who wants to go for a ride?" was always met with great excitement. A happy tail would whip about wildly, and just in case you ever forgot where his leash was, Luke was eager to point out where it hung. His rides in the car were always exciting. On this particular day, a surprise meeting would make things even more exciting.

A slew of vehicles with trees affixed firmly to roofs or stuffed inside hatchbacks filled a farm lot. Families with saws all looked to participate in the holiday tradition. Some rode by tractor pulling a wagon and others waded through a sea of trees. We set off into the man-made forest that provided temporary homes to many birds and small animals. This was a feast of smells for Luke to follow—row after row and tree to tree, so many things to explore. The wafting smell of burning wood filled the air.

As we made our way along the rows looking for that special tree, Luke sniffed, poked, and prodded, never forgetting to mark along the way. He ignored those lowly built nests and small chipmunk dens, pointing as dogs do to a nearby outdoor pen. His ears were back and his stare direct as he spied something new. Looking back from an enclosure pen was a creature snorting a howdy-do. This strange sight wearing bells and a red blanket caused Luke to tilt his head.

The sniffing bounced back and forth, each beast catching a scent riding just above the smell of burning pine and hot chocolate. Luke held his ground, performing his best version of "the point": body straight with front leg lifted. The other creature shook his head, bells chiming, and pawed at the frozen ground. Although they never could have previously met, they acted as if they had. A whine and a huff from Luke to us showed his deep interest.

Twice Luke's height with weight to match and a head adorned with furry antlers, this wasn't Rudolph, Donner, Blitzen, or any of Santa's elite. But this was a reindeer greeting people. A rugged sign said his name was Pete. Luke pulled at his leash, wanting to get a closer look at this fascinating new fella. We walked Luke up so that dog and reindeer could meet each other. Luke was submissive and maybe a little scared, but they sniffed nose-to-nose, eye-to-eye, and you could see the interest between the two. I would love to embellish and say that they ran, pranced, and played together in holiday joy, but that wasn't the case. But it was something special to see their curiosity play out before us.

We finally had to force a break between these two to seek our perfect tree. But Luke kept straining his neck toward the pen to see his new friend. With our tree cut, bundled, and secured, Luke took one last look back at Pete. A treat was needed to motivate Luke for the ride home, but once he was in the back seat, he was content to sprawl out on our tree. His pitty mug had a smile stretched across it. What was he thinking? Maybe it was about the birds, squirrels, or critters found. Maybe it was about his time spent with his family pack and his ride back home. Or maybe that smile came from his meeting an odd and unusual friend beyond the sea of pines.

Luke has now passed over the rainbow bridge, and he left us with many great memories and experiences. I like to think that as he replayed his best moments in his doggy dreams, he often went back to that tree farm to visit his antlered friend—maybe sharing a bark, a snort, or a mutual sniff. That year's Christmas season holds a moment I will always cherish and remember—when Luke the dog met Pete the reindeer.

19

Love at First Sight

Jeff Adams

G et up!" My wife, Rosemary, shook me. "We have to go." She pulled back the covers. "Now."

"Go where?"

"I found your present."

"It's Christmas Eve morning." I looked at the clock. "Who's open at seven o'clock?"

"Never mind. Just get dressed. We have to drive clear across the valley to Tempe."

"Why?" I rubbed my eyes. "Don't they have a store on the west side?"

"No. One location only. Here are your pants. Hurry up."

"Well, give them a credit card."

"Cash only. Come on."

I scratched my head. *What kind of business doesn't take credit cards?* "Ask them to hold it; we'll go right after breakfast."

"They won't hold it. I already asked. I saw the ad in this morning's paper. I called. There's one left. That's it. It's now or never. I've been looking for two months."

I stumbled into my clothes. *At least there's not much traffic.* It still took almost an hour to drive across Phoenix on the freeways.

"Get off at the next exit," Rosemary said. "Go to Target."

"I thought you said they didn't take credit cards."

"Your present is not at Target. But if I take you with me, you'll know what it is as soon as I pull up. Get out. Hurry."

I stepped out of our little S-10 pickup. Rosemary climbed behind the steering wheel and sped away as the door closed. *Bye.*

I went inside Target and ordered a hot tea and some sort of pastry and a couple of cookies. *Breakfast of champions.*

I had no idea how long I'd be stuck waiting for Rosemary to come back. I played Sherlock Holmes. *What could she possibly get that's one of a kind at a store that only takes cash?* I thought of old books. She'd given me a first-edition *Winnie-the-Pooh* a few years earlier. *But I didn't include the titles of any old books on my wish list.* Maybe she found an old film, but I'd only listed recent releases that I'd seen in a theater. I looked up just in time to see Rosemary walking through the doors.

"I need to get a bow," she said.

"Really, you don't. You don't even have to wrap it."

"That's good. It's too big. I'll be right back."

I finished my last cookie and waited for her to return.

"Let's go," Rosemary said, bag in hand. "But you have to close your eyes."

"I promise I won't peek. Just put it behind the seat."

"I told you, it's too big."

"Then put it in the bed of the truck."

"I can't. It might fall out." She waved her hand in front of my face. "Don't spoil the surprise. Take my arm." I put my hand on her elbow and hoped I wouldn't trip.

We walked across the parking lot. "Stop. Wait here. Close your eyes." I held on to the tailgate. I never saw or heard or smelled anything. "Now, a few more steps. Turn. Open your eyes."

Staring at my face from the front seat of my truck were the biggest, softest brown eyes I'd ever seen. With a big red bow stuck on her bigger-than-normal boxy head, the girl of my dreams gazed at me. I leaned forward to touch her nose with mine as I held that gorgeous golden retriever face in my hands. Tears rolled over my cheeks. A couple stood near another pickup truck. "They wanted to see," Rosemary said.

"Our son is going to college. He can't take her," the wife said. "They're not allowed pets in a dorm. He's had her since she was weaned when he was twelve years old."

"Your wife was the first one to call us—before seven o'clock," the husband said. "This was the first day the ad ran. She was a birthday present for our son. Now she's a Christmas present."

"They've been inseparable all these years," the mom said. "We wanted to meet the man who's going to love her."

"Oh, I do."

"I think it's love at first sight," the dad said.

"What's her name?" I asked.

"Bear," Rosemary said.

"Bear." I turned my attention to my new love. "You're gorgeous." I'd wanted a golden retriever for more years than I could remember. I couldn't take my eyes off her. "She's so beautiful. So gentle."

The couple dabbed at their tears. "You can't pet her too much," said the mother. Bear slipped her cold wet nose under my hand and flipped her head up. "That's what she does when she wants to be petted, which is all the time."

Although she had the credentials of an AKC registered pure-bred, I knew she would never win a prize in any show. Her lower teeth jutted out because of an underbite. Her front paws turned in and her hind legs pointed outward. I didn't care. I didn't want her for show. I wanted her because I needed unconditional love.

"Ready, girl?"

I lifted her off the tailgate. Rosemary would drive. Bear and I would snuggle. She spilled off my legs and onto the floor of the cab.

"She needs a collar and a leash," Rosemary said. "They told me she's trained." I didn't care if she obeyed my commands, except for the sake of safety. At the pet store, Bear chose her food and a few toys—including a bone and a ball—along with a box of treats. We showed her different colors and styles of leashes and collars. "She doesn't seem to have a preference," I noted.

"Pink?" Rosemary asked.

"Red, I think. She's big and bold."

"And beautiful."

"Beautimus Maximus," I said. "Her name in Latin: Houndus Dogus Beautimus Maximus."

Bear tugged on the leash as if to tell me, "Come on, boy. You need a walk."

Back at the house again, we played outside. I'd throw the ball and Bear would stare at me. Rosemary interpreted. "She's saying, 'You threw it, you get it.'" So I did. She was golden but she didn't retrieve.

I don't remember any other presents I got for Christmas that year. I didn't need anything else. I had the one thing I'd wanted since we were married eight years earlier.

Over Bear's years with us, there would be times I had to leave her side, but she never left my heart. We moved to Las Vegas and she endured me being at work all day. But whenever Rosemary and I went out for dinner, Bear would find something that belonged to Rosemary to send an unmistakable message. Wadded up in the middle of the living room floor, we'd find a scarf or whatever Bear chose to desecrate—sopping wet. Not chewed or destroyed, just coated in dog saliva. Rosemary understood. "She's saying, 'You and me, boy, we make beautiful music together. But the fat chick has gotta go.'"

Eventually, Bear accepted Rosemary as a friend. Or at least she tolerated Rosemary. Maybe because my wife would walk with her around our neighborhood. Perhaps in Bear's mind that wasn't necessary. But the law stated that a dog "must be on a leash and under control."

We learned that fact one day when an animal control officer slowed and stopped and stared. "That your dog?" Rosemary nodded. The man cited the statute from memory, and then looked at Bear waiting patiently with her leash still in her mouth. "Looks like she knows. On a leash and under control. Have a nice day, ma'am."

A 5.0 earthquake with its epicenter only a few miles away roused Bear only enough to cause her to lift her head and then plop it down again. My friend John nicknamed her Chalkline for the outline around a dead body. She may not have moved fast, but she permanently moved my life from the first moment.

Sometimes love doesn't wait because it can't wait; it comes to you. Sometimes we're loved first, before we can love in return. Sometimes we're loved before we can do anything that would make us lovable. Sometimes we're loved before we know it—at first sight.

20

The Sweater
That Would Not Be

Chrissy Drew

C'mon, it will keep you warm, Tanner."

Tanner is my rescue pup, and I do everything in my power to spoil him.

After I retired, it soon became clear I had no real purpose in my day-to-day. Scrolling through social media on my phone seemed to be my hobby. One I was not happy about. I believe this pup rescued me; I needed him. Though I didn't know if a puppy fit into my relaxing routine, God's plan was different.

I made sure the rescue center and foster fur-parents knew I wanted a small lapdog. I sure got one. We believe he's a Chihuahua/ Italian whippet. If you don't know much about short-haired dogs, especially Chihuahuas, they chill and shiver even if it doesn't seem cold. After witnessing his uncontrollable shaking the first time, I took him shopping to our nearest pet store and purchased a winter-design sweater.

Upon arriving home, I ripped open the packaging as Tanner looked on. Maybe I was overly excited to put this doggie apparel on him. He appeared more curious about price tags and labels.

Getting him to settle down would be another story. As he sniffed this piece of green knit with snowflake designs, I could see this wasn't going to be as easy as I'd hoped. Much to my dismay, he assumed he'd be getting another chew toy. He would not sit still on my lap. He twisted and spun around, trying to snatch the sweater out of my hands. This six-month-old whippet had way too much energy. I kept thinking, *How am I going to keep up with him?*

I managed to get the sweater over his large pointed ears and through his long thin legs. I was excited to see what he'd do. But he appeared anxious and was still shaking and squirming. No sooner did I set him down in the backyard than he began leaping in circles, biting and gnawing at the sweater, trying to pull it over his head. He looked like a bucking bronco. Evidently whippets love jumping . . . high. I became fearful he'd land wrong on those skinny little legs.

I watched for a few moments, laughing so hard as the sweater covered his eyes. I scooped him up and yanked it completely off his hard-breathing body. *That seemed easier than putting it on,* I thought.

I knew I wouldn't be able to force him to wear the sweater. Disappointed, I carried Tanner back inside, hugging him close. I was bummed I couldn't take the sweater back, as he'd chewed a hole in it. Thankfully, I got a video of this day's antics.

Christmas rolled around, and Tanner received a present from his cousin, Stanley the cat, via my sissy. I gave him the wrapped gift, and he tore into it, paper flying.

"Oh no," I exclaimed. "Another sweater." He shook it, viciously. I don't think he could believe it either. I wondered if dogs have memories. This would be his second warm piece of knit I'd try on him. I could have sworn I told my sissy about his first sweater ordeal. She forgot. Though I was hesitant, my conscience worked on me, the sweater being a gift and all. Plus, his shivering on this cold December day broke my heart.

I pried the sweater out of his little snappy mouth. He jumped three feet trying to snatch it out of my hand. My little whippet. No one told me about this breed's jumping traits. Would have been nice to be prepared, though I'm not certain what I could have done about it.

I waited awhile to put it on his overexcited self. When I say waited, I mean several days before retrieving the sweater from its hiding place where he couldn't see or smell it. And, this particular day, I decided to try just as he awakened from his long puppy nap.

"Okay, buddy. Mommy wants you to be warm. Let's try this pretty blue sweater." Not like he knows colors, of course. But I converse with him daily. I like to think my voice calms him.

Until he saw it.

I expertly put it over his head and through his legs before he had a chance to complain . . . much. Without delay, he began trying to pull it off.

The battle commenced.

Once again, I carried my squirming pup outdoors and set him down, and once again, the bucking bronco showed up. Jumping up, kicking his legs out, chewing, and trying to pull the sweater over his head. I laughed out loud. I can only imagine what my neighbors thought, although they must have been used to it by then. They saw me laugh with my dog every day. He makes my heart smile.

I pulled him up, went indoors, took the sweater off, and tossed it in the trash.

"I tried, Tanner, but you just aren't having it."

When Sissy asked about Tanner's Christmas gift, instead of telling her, I texted my video. All she could do was laugh. I told her to tell Stanley the cat not to send any more clothing items to his cousin. She agreed.

I'd like to be able to keep him warm outside. Sometimes I walk through our pet store and wonder if there's anything he'd wear to alleviate his shivering. It's a fleeting thought. I know it will never happen.

But then I got to thinking. He won't wear sweaters to keep his body warm and in fact hates putting his paws on wet, dewy grass. Maybe . . . puppy booties?

21

Sam and Caiou

Connie Webster

The year was 1958, just thirteen years after the end of WWII. It was an innocent, hope-filled time. It was the year of the Hula Hoop. The president was Dwight D. Eisenhower, and the baby boom was still in an upswing.

Dick, my oldest brother, was eleven, my sister, Janet, ten, and Carl was eight. I was six. Though my family was quite poor, we were very fortunate to be living with the basic necessities of life on thirty acres of cornfields, woods, and swamps in southern Michigan. My parents were able to purchase the property after scrimping and saving while my father worked as a truck driver and my mother as a waitress. My father drew the plans himself for our small house, and every free moment my parents had was filled with working on this home of their dreams, struggling to build it from the ground up as they were able to finance each step.

The basement was first. The six of us moved into it that summer in order to cut costs and so Mom and Dad could work on the house whenever time allowed. The basement was the only semifinished area of the house at that time at roughly 26-by-20 feet with a wall running the length of it just left of center, dividing it into two sides. The narrower side served as entry, kitchen, dining room, bath, and pantry. The larger side was living area and sleep space for all six of us.

Mom stretched sheets across the far end of the room in order to make a separation between their bed, which also served as a couch of sorts in this unique living arrangement, and the two twin beds, which made up the sleeping arrangement for us four kids. It was tight living quarters at a time well before the "tiny house" idea was a thing.

The upstairs of the house was a shell at this point, just studs reaching for the stars. In my mind it looked like the empty rib cage of a giant dinosaur. My brothers and sister and I, with the keen imaginations of our youth, scrambled around the first-floor, subflooring level, balancing on two-by-fours and cement blocks, envisioning our bedrooms, pretending to fill our closets and settle our spaces.

This summer was a wonderful time for the four of us kids. We ran about the land, investigating our new world. The four seasons are lovely in Michigan, but I believe that fall is especially beautiful with Michigan's variety of trees and waterways. As the temperatures dropped, we started wearing our shoes outdoors. We found an abundance of walnut trees along the border of our property, so we went about collecting the walnuts, staining our hands and clothes in the process and causing our mother much frustration. Dad helped us shuck them, then set them aside to dry and cure before we were able to finally crack them and enjoy their delicious insides.

Fall gave way to winter, and the snows came down and blanketed our world in pristine beauty. The change in our surroundings was magical. Of course, with the snow, my mind turned to thoughts of Christmas and the excitement of this, our first Christmas huddled in the basement of our new home.

It was meager, but Mom and Dad made Christmas a special time. Dad and we four kids trudged through the deepening snow to find and cut down the perfect tree, small and nearly cylindrical so as not to overwhelm our small living/sleeping space. We decorated our tiny sweet-smelling tree with homemade ornaments, and it truly looked magical to me with its string of lights the only source of light in our living space. Of course, Mom wanted to be able to see in the house, but when allowed, I would turn off all the lamps and enjoy that lovely little tree with its quiet light.

We were told that on that Christmas morning, we could only open our Christmas stockings before Mom and Dad joined us. So my brothers and sister and I woke up early and tiptoed past Mom and Dad's bed to where our stockings hung on the wall beside our little tree. When Mom and Dad finally got up, we jumped up on their bed and enjoyed the candy from our stockings and opened the few gifts gathered under the tree. When all the opening of gifts appeared to be done, Dad excused himself and stepped out the door. He returned quickly with a box that was actually bouncing in his hands and making strange sounds. When he set it down in the middle of the floor, I noticed a little black nose popping through the opening on top. We all shouted in unison, "Puppies!"

Sure enough, as my eldest brother opened the box, out popped a squirming black lab mix puppy. Next a tiny beagle puppy the color of butterscotch came tumbling out. We were over the top with excitement, and after lots of play and some hours we decided on names for them. Our playful black lab mix male would be Sam. Our sweet little beagle, who made the most lovely, mournful sounds, was named Caiou, because that name most closely resembled the sound of her call. Of course, they were mutts, and I'm guessing that our father found them at no cost from a neighbor. But Mom and Dad couldn't have given us a better gift. Sam and Caiou were our happy companions for many years as we investigated our wild thirty acres, running through the woods, finding turtles and frogs, building forts, picking wild berries, and living happy, carefree lives.

I have many wonderful memories of Christmases through the years. But Sam and Caiou, those free, mixed-breed puppies, were the happiest and most memorable gifts of my childhood.

22

Christmas Presence— Lily and Luca

Marian McConnell

Several years ago, my daughter, Molly, adopted a rescue Belgian Malinois whom she named Luca, which means light. This is a working breed known for their intelligence and agility, especially as bomb-sniffers for police and the military.

Luca looked like a miniature German shepherd, fifty pounds of smarts and strength with a beautiful coat of tan, mahogany, and black, and a tiny white heart shape on his chest. His fur was thick and his tail a gorgeous curl waving behind him. His dark chocolate eyes looked at you intently, and he was a great listener. Even Molly's fiancé, who didn't think he liked dogs, fell in love with Luca. The three of them became inseparable.

Molly and our "granddog," Luca, celebrated the Christmas season that first year with visits to our home. One of my favorite videos is the one I took of Molly showing off all the tricks she had taught Luca, while her favorite movie, *The Sound of Music*, plays in the background. Luca performed all his tricks—sit, stay, roll over, high five, shake, lay, speak—eagerly. Their bond was a joy to behold.

"I know you'll get another dog," Molly told her father and me. She said this despite our vows to have no more pets. A couple of years earlier, my husband, Dano, and I had had to put down our thirteen-year-old black lab. Since then, we didn't want to take on another dog, much less the certain pain of losing one.

That next summer Dano and I rode our Harleys a thousand miles from our home in Virginia to the Ozarks. Although we were in our midsixties, we still enjoyed riding our motorcycles, and we took trips all over the USA. My bike was a 2013 Harley Davidson Softail Deluxe I called "Scarlett O'Harley" because we love to be "gone with the wind." Molly preferred horses and had a way with them like she had with dogs. Dano and I preferred "iron" horses and loved the thrill of visiting new places and the camaraderie of other bikers and friends made along the way.

On this trip, we pulled in to our favorite motel not far from Eureka Springs, Arkansas. A little pit-terrier mix with a brindle coat and white markings ran up to us as if she knew us. About thirty pounds, not quite a year old, she had a white stripe down her forehead, white cowl around her neck, white feet, and a white-tipped tail. Her big, bat-like ears showed her mood depending on what she was doing—running (she was superfast), begging for a piece of whatever we were eating, or making new friends. A little pink on her nose and a pink belly made her especially endearing.

We learned the dog had been abandoned there about three months prior by a young woman who had asked an elderly man who lived near the motel to feed her for a few days. The man told me her name was Lily. The owner never returned, so the man continued to feed the dog, and in really cold weather let her come into his house. He had never taken her to a vet or made any attempt to adopt her, hoping someone would eventually claim her.

This sweet dog immediately attached herself to us, following us everywhere, sleeping outside our motel room, and accompanying me on my morning jogs. Despite our vow to remain dogless, Lily's exuberance and friendliness melted our resolve.

She was brave too—there were about sixty other motorcycles there for the rally we were attending, and the noise and movements of the bikes didn't faze her a bit. During the rally, bike games were held. One game, "Road Kill," has biker couples take turns with the man in front riding the bike slowly as the woman on the back uses a large fishing net to scoop up "road kill"— actually little stuffed animal toys—from the parking lot. The couple who scoops up the most animals wins.

When it was our turn, I was scooping when one of the stuffed animals fell out of the net. Lily came running out of the crowd, picked up the animal, and carried it behind our bike until we stopped so she could give it to me. We may not have won the contest, but Lily got the crowd's biggest cheer.

By the third day Dano said, "If we can find a vet to check her over and give her whatever shots she needs, and if we can find a safe way to get her to Virginia, I'll say yes to this dog. Lily is special." We found a transport system and a local vet who administered her shots and told us she was healthy and fit to travel. She arrived at her forever home within a week's time.

Back home, we were overwhelmed with Lily's unconditional love. Her whole body wiggled with joy when she was with us. She was friendly and accepting of everyone, including other dogs. She was so well-behaved and sociable that she was allowed to come to work with me at the local homeless shelter, a refuge for men, women, and children. She made many friends there and soon had her own unofficial fan club.

From the first time I took Lily to see Molly and Luca, the pups became instant buddies. It became a monthly tradition to visit them in Charlottesville and have mother-daughter time while the pups raced and tumbled and played in the dog park in front of the house. When Molly and Luca visited us in Catawba, we would all take walks in our woods, hike the Appalachian Trail, and explore local waterfalls.

"I knew it! I knew y'all would get another dog," Molly would say with a grin. She'd hug Lily to her one side and Luca to her other. This was one time Dano and I were glad to be wrong and to freely admit she was right.

We celebrated Christmas Eve at Molly's that year. My last picture of her was her and her fiancé standing by their little Christmas tree with homemade ornaments and both pups playing at their feet. Molly's eyes glittered, and she grinned from ear to ear.

Molly and I talked on the phone on Christmas. She was not feeling well. She was dealing with chronic pain caused by endometriosis, something she suffered with every month since she was thirteen years old. Together we had searched for ways to deal with this debilitating pain. She tried different doctors, drugs, acupuncture, yoga, meditation, and the last few years an herbal regimen. Luca was an especially amazing source of comfort to her during those rough times. Molly would make some hot herbal tea and crawl under a heavy quilt, and Luca would lay next to her with his nose across her lap, looking up at her with liquid brown eyes of compassion and total devotion.

I sent a text expressing my mom worry. The last text I got from Molly was on December 29. She told me she loved me and signed off with a smiley face. I knew her fiancé and Luca would take care of her. They always did with compassion and love.

But the Christmas season will never be the same for us, because we lost Molly on New Year's Day. It was a tragic, unfathomable loss, related to her years of chronic pain. We believe some of the remedies she was using to combat it blurred her ability to fight an impulse to end her pain permanently. And so, she was gone. She was only thirty-one years old. We were all in shock, including Luca and Lily. Even they were somber and quiet. There had been a shift in our universe, and a light had gone out in our world when Molly took flight to heaven.

Since then, our Christmas tree stays up all year with ornaments of Molly and angels gracing the branches twinkling with built-in LED lights. Lily takes turns sitting in our laps in our oversized chairs, all forty-two pounds of her reminding us of happy times, unconditional love, and how precious life is. Dano and I love and support each other in human ways, but I can't tell you how many tears I have cried into Lily's fur and all the sharing I have done with her about my grief and loss. Lily never judges or questions. She just listens and loves me back.

We know for sure Lily came to us for a reason—not just to be rescued, but to rescue us. There are no words for the loss of a child. The bond between a mother and daughter is sacred. We were part of each other, and now there is a hole in my soul that only she could fill. We always appreciate when family and friends say, "I am so sorry for your loss." It's respectful and helps keep Molly's memory alive.

But Lily has truly been a godsend to me, because she seems to sense that loss and will just "be there" for me. I stroke her fur, take long walks in our woods where we used to walk with Molly and Luca, and sit in the evenings with her warm body on my lap. She keeps me grounded in what was, what is, and what will someday be. She gives the same comfort to Dano, and we take turns sharing love and memories back and forth and all around.

We stay in touch with Molly's fiancé and Luca, and we still visit. Lily and Luca still love each other like a brother and sister, and we all watch them play in the park.

Recently I painted a picture in honor of Molly. It's of Luca and Lily, à la *Lady and the Tramp*, the Disney movie of two dogs who fall in love. It's from our favorite scene of them sharing a spaghetti noodle. I imagine Molly smiling at this over my shoulder.

We feel Molly's love all around us, and we know eventually we will all be together. (Yes, I do believe dogs go to heaven too.) We will forever be grateful for Lily and Luca, especially on Christmas. Their presence in our lives is our very best present.

23

To Grandfather's House We Go

Rhonda Dragomir

A streak of black-and-tan fur flew up Dad's basement stairs and leaped into my lap without breaking stride. The puppy licked my face and moved on to his next victim, leaving behind a wet stream from his overexcited bladder.

"Now you've met Samson!" Dad chuckled at my distress as I went to change clothing.

Greg, a friend who rented my parents' basement apartment, had adopted Samson. The puppy had been brought to the homeless shelter where Greg worked by a kind rescuer who found him discarded in a paper bag on an interstate highway.

Captivated by Samson's bright eyes and friendly demeanor, my father loved the dog just as much as Greg did. Who could resist a mongrel sporting the black tongue of a chow chow, the coloring of a coonhound, and the luxurious fur of a spaniel? Samson's handsome appearance and winning personality sparked Dad's comments that he should be the father of a new AKC breed.

Puppy play highlighted our Kentucky Christmas visit that year, and on the way home, our daughter begged for a wooly playmate of her own. Our beloved cats had both passed away, and the house seemed lonely without a furry companion. Though considering the possibility, we didn't rush into dog ownership. My husband's father was terminally ill, and we needed to be able to travel at a moment's notice.

Our summons came less than a week later, and we journeyed to Ohio to be with my father-in-law in his last days. Dale, my husband, sought me in the kitchen of his family home one day. Smiles were hard to come by as we grieved, but one corner of his mouth lifted slightly. He had received a phone call about Samson.

Greg worked extensive hours at the shelter, and he was disturbed to leave Samson for long, lonely days in his outdoor kennel. The dog was too boisterous for my disabled father to handle, and Mom had no desire to clean up puppy droppings. Samson needed a new home, and Greg accurately perceived that we would love and care for him.

After relating the details of the call, Dale asked a startling question. "Honey, how would you feel about getting a dog?"

It was the absolute worst time to make such an important decision. But our dog-loving family needed a boost of joy, so we agreed. When we arrived home in North Carolina after the funeral, Greg and Samson met us there. We welcomed the change. Caring for the dog and adapting to new routines brightened our season of sorrow.

But a big problem soon manifested. Samson had grown so much in the days since we had seen him that our six-year-old couldn't walk the brute on a leash. He lived up to his biblical namesake, dragging her around the yard with his unearthly strength.

"Names have meaning, you know, and Samson needs a new name. He's strong all right, but he's also stubborn." Dale's solemn pronouncement was not unexpected. As a pastor, he had studied both Hebrew and Greek and often featured name meanings in his sermons.

After rejecting several other Bible names, we finally agreed on Bendito, which means "little blessing" in Spanish and seemed appropriate for a spaniel mix. Though Bendito quickly outgrew the "little," he lived up to the rest of his new name, blessing us with a big heart full of devotion to his new family.

Soon his name was shortened to Ben, and we morphed into a dog-centered household. Maturing to weigh more than fifty pounds, Ben gleefully ignored obedience lessons. He never mastered the mannerly art of canine walking, maxing out whatever leash we used despite wearing a choke collar. He panted, snuffled, and galloped wildly through yards, greeting one and all with the same exuberance he bestowed on family members.

And heaven help us should he escape the house unleashed! A wild look would flare in his eyes, and he'd dart after squirrels, neighborhood children on bikes, and—to our horror—even the occasional vehicle. Ben trained church members to ring the parsonage doorbell and stand back a step or two until we corralled him. Greetings took place outdoors as often as possible because he never outgrew his puppy habit of sprinkling visitors.

Our annual trek to my parents' house for Christmas had usually been comprised of 350 miles of yawns, sleepy driver swaps, and unending queries of, "Are we there yet?" Ben changed that paradigm on his first trip. He reveled in car rides, especially if any part of his body could be in contact with Dale, his pack leader. Sometimes he nodded off, but when we parked and turned off the engine, he sprang into action, panting and barking to exit the minivan.

At one rest stop, I surveyed the wreckage in the back seat. My artfully wrapped gifts were trampled, and bags of snacks had been crushed to crumbs. I grumbled that if any happy people traveled over the river and through the woods to Grandmother's house, they likely towed the dog behind their one-horse open sleigh.

We got a late start that Christmas Eve, not uncommon for us. The church's children's nativity play and fellowship dinner had taken place the night before, and we were understandably a little weary. We would arrive home much later than I wanted, but I began to cheer up in the gloaming hour when Christmas lights winked from porches and yards. A light dusting of snow added to the picture-postcard scenery, and the sound system hummed with selections from my vast collection of holiday music.

With the descent of darkness, Ben calmed. He lay contented and drowsy between our bucket seats. Mom and Dad had visited us that summer, so we knew he would remember them, but we wondered how he would react to seeing his home from puppy days.

Two long hills graced the two-lane road into my hometown, and excitement added to my thrill of floating over each apex. Our daughter and the dog slept peacefully as we made the final turn into the subdivision where my parents live.

Many previous turns on our journey had not disturbed Ben one iota. He moved nary a muscle on any corner the entire day until the engine was turned off. But on that final turn, the dog woke and went berserk. He hopped and barked, vaulting onto the lap of our daughter, who startled awake with a cry. Panting and whining, he pressed his snout to the windows, leaving a trail of doggy mucus and fog.

Thankfully, only two blocks remained to reach our destination. We pulled up in front of the house and parked. Mom and Dad's sidewalk led straight to the front door, which was open in anticipation of our arrival. Through the entrance, I spied Dad in his favorite spot—his oversized recliner.

So did Ben.

The dog's excitement presented a danger to anything between him and Dad, so Dale simply flung open the minivan door. Ben exploded from the vehicle as if he'd been launched from a cannon, and there was no romp through the neighborhood, leash or no leash. He had one destination in mind.

Mom opened the glass storm door just before Hurricane Ben struck, sparing it the brunt of landfall. The dog zoomed past her with a friendly yip, but he knew where he most wanted to be. He sailed through the air with a Samson-like leap and smothered Dad with canine kisses, eliciting oomphs from my father. Tummy trampling was a much bigger ordeal when performed by a mature dog instead of a puppy.

When Ben calmed to tropical storm strength, we told my parents of his innate sense that he was nearing his former home. God must have created him with internal GPS. We could not explain how he knew, and he would always exhibit the same behavior at the same spot on every subsequent trip.

After we finished hugs and greetings all around on that memorable Christmas Eve, it was time to relax and enjoy our vacation.

I did relish a little sweet revenge from the previous year.

This time, Dad had to get up and change his clothes.

24

The Gift of Dog

Lisa Begin-Kruysman

The Christmas season conjures up traditional visions of mangers and mistletoe and the sounds of musical medleys of holiday favorites. In many households, however, the season is also filled with the persistent requests that a new puppy be left under the tree come Christmas morning.

Such was the case in my childhood home one Christmas. Although as an adult, I've come to understand the downside of pets received as holiday gifts, the almost-ten-year-old me was oblivious. A born dog-lover, I'd spent enough time bonding with the toy poodles owned by family friends—tiny little bits of fluff the color of a Hershey's Kiss—to know I wanted one of my own.

Eventually, my Christmas campaign for a canine was successful. My parents, worn down, contacted a toy poodle breeder. As luck would have it, the puppies would be available by the time of my birthday, conveniently three weeks after Christmas. I was informed by my parents that due to the cost of a purebred dog, this gift would be a combo Christmas/birthday gift. I didn't care if it counted for the next decade of birthday gifts.

I was blissful in my hard-won victory. Everything from that point on became a blur. Skip the stockings. No visits to see Santa—no problem. The only month that mattered to me was January, when I'd turn ten and become a dog owner. Finally.

In mid-January the big day arrived. A tiny eight-week-old toy poodle named Coco Puff snuggled in my welcoming arms. It was an exciting time, and at first everyone in my family wanted to care for her. Unfortunately, the sensitive and fragile Coco was not a good match for our rough-and-tumble household complete with four kids, their friends, and forty-plus cousins. She reacted to our family circus by becoming snarly, snippy, and nippy. Her daily care—brushing, feeding, walking—often fell to my parents as Coco came to distrust children.

But I loved her. She'd been *my* gift, and from fifth grade to my senior year of high school, Coco remained my dog. When she died, it was so traumatic for me that it would be nearly twenty-five years before I'd have another dog.

On September 11, 2001, I was working in my artist studio at the New Jersey Shore when my morning radio programming was interrupted. A plane had crashed into one of the World Trade Center towers. I recall thinking this was no accident and went inside to turn on televised news and watched as the horrific events began to unfold.

Alone at home, I felt helpless. Most of my neighbors were at work, and my husband, Rich, immersed in his darkroom at his place of employment, was puzzled by my urgent phone call about a plane crash.

I thought how comforting it would be to have a dog by my side—an excuse to venture out and explore the neighborhood just to bond with someone who was also watching the escalating and terrifying news. In the numbing weeks that followed, my need for the comfort of a dog increased, and a new adult version of the campaign for a canine emerged. This time my husband would need convincing.

While watching a program on Animal Planet, I was captivated by a segment on Portuguese water dogs. This unique non-shedding breed had served as constant companions to boaters and fishermen throughout the ages. My campaign focus became tighter; I'd convince my water-loving husband that we needed a robust, fun-loving Portie (as they are known) in our lives.

Finding one was not easy, however, for at that time Porties were considered a rare breed. With careful research, however, I was able to locate a breeder just twenty minutes from our home. A phone call led to an interview and the news that one of the breeder's dogs was expecting a new litter on, or very near, Christmas day.

The day after Christmas we commenced our drive to Orlando, Florida, to visit Universal Studios. A day later we received the news that the puppies had been born! Nine in all—three of them female. We were told the females were spoken for, so we'd be getting one of the males.

While standing in line at the *Jaws* attraction, Rich announced that he wanted to name our new pup Hooper after the Matt Hooper character in the *Jaws* movie played by Richard Dreyfus. Hooper? Why not Quint or Brody? Happy that he remained excited about welcoming a new dog, I obliged, filing the other names away for future dogs.

During several visits to the breeder's home, it was made clear to Rich and me that Porties were not easy dogs due to their intelligence and willfulness. Undaunted, in April on Easter Sunday, we welcomed Hooper into our home. The breeder surprised us with the female we'd originally requested. She appeared to be a snuggly sweetie, but the words of one of the breeder's sons remained with me as we'd left with our dog. "Of all the puppies in the litter, she's the most difficult."

I'd quickly find out that he was probably right. On her first night with us, Hooper stared up at me with her amber eyes (Portie eye contact is intense) before she walked over to her empty food bowl and shoved it toward me with her paw, requesting more. During our early leash walks, she'd circle around me with such speed that her paws barely touched the ground. She was nick-named the Black Tornado by a concerned neighbor who watched our vigorous walks.

In the coming years, Hooper's exuberance only intensified. She was a skilled counter-surfer, and one Thanksgiving while we all dined, she claimed the still meaty turkey carcass for herself. Getting caught red-pawed, she dragged the carcass across my sister's beautiful hardwood floors in a failed attempt to keep her prize. The stain and memory are permanent. She hid in the back of a deep, dark closet at a condo we'd rented in Florida, ignoring our pleas and calls for two days because she feared another road trip. She'd confiscate the phone from the crick of my neck as I multitasked, pilfered entire blocks of cheese, chewed up countless books, purses, and sweaters, and one time she broke up a party on someone's boat by heaving a large mound of undigested kibble on deck just as the hors d'oeuvres were served.

Our Hoop Girl had many a "Marley moment." But she was loving and loyal. She adored Rich and small children.

At age eleven, Hooper's health took a sudden turn, and we did the hardest thing a pet owner must do. My last words to Hooper still live clearly in my memory. I spoke softly to her and requested that when the time was right, she'd send a new furry friend to comfort us. But I also asked that the new dog be mellow because, although the breeder promised me Hooper would calm down by age three, she never really did. It seemed like an odd thing to ask of a beloved dog, but I didn't want to become one of those people who in their grief vowed never to have another dog.

Not long after, superstorm Sandy ravaged our neighborhood. Our home was spared, but many of my neighbors were forced to live elsewhere. That Christmas was a dark one, literally—no trees twinkling in windows, no bright and sparkling lights, and for us, no silly dog to dress up in a Santa hat to pose for photos or sing happy birthday to.

I thought it would be nice to foster dogs to fill the void of our empty home. The first two were pretty easy. They came and went within days. But then the online image of a little black-and-white dog melted my heart. I asked to foster him, and despite great odds, in early January, a Havanese mix named Teddy met us on the highway via transport.

He'd arrived with a pile of applications from people eager to adopt him, but as he spent more time with us, it became clear he was adopting us. The pile of adoption papers was shredded. I believed Hooper had somehow sent Teddy to us as a gift when we needed one most.

Teddy has been an incredible gift—in times of darkness a shining star as bright as the stars in a cold winter night sky or a glowing Christmas tree topper in a window. I often share with Teddy tales of Hooper's antics. Teddy, as mellow as a Sunday morning, isn't impressed. He typically responds with a yawn and a stretch.

The gift of dog is that they remind us that there is no time like the present and no present like time. In a dog's presence, every day can hold all the hope and happiness of a lifetime of Christmas mornings. And maybe a future with a Quint or Brody too.

25

The Countess Arrived

Chris Kent

My husband and I were closing in on a retirement date. Just a couple months away from the freedom to do what we wanted, when we wanted to do it. One day, in passing, my husband happened to mention a colleague of ours at work whose dog had a litter of puppies—German shorthair. "Let's go see them."

I know the rule: you never take a child to see a litter of puppies if you aren't planning to bring one home. I suspected that I should not agree to go with my husband, a bird hunter, to see a litter of bird dogs. But we already had a dog, a black lab, so I was confident he wasn't thinking about another dog.

We broke the rule—because yes, we brought home a puppy. He was special. We often said he was quite possibly a once-in-a-lifetime companion. Kaiser was a black-and-white German shorthair. Smart, loyal, devoted, steadfast, athletic, but also mischievous. You knew if you put your hat down, he would have it in a second, with a game of "Catch Me If You Can" underway. He would race a four-wheeler, point and flush a grouse, and snuggle next to you on the couch. Kaiser was a friend and companion who shared our life and love for almost fourteen years. On a sad day in early December, we had to let him go. We loved him until the end.

After that, the days in our house were quiet—too quiet. We sat there expecting a scratch at the door that never came. We expected to hear the clicking of his nails on the hardwood floor but instead heard only silence. We expected him to be next to us on the couch, but he wasn't there. At night he should have been curled at our feet in bed. The thought of replacing him, finding a puppy, seemed to desecrate his memory. He couldn't be replaced. But at the same time, could we live our remaining years without a canine companion?

Without saying anything to my husband, I started to search the internet for kennels. I knew if we got another dog, we wanted a shorthair, black and white, but I thought it should be a girl so she would not be compared to Kaiser. Nothing came up during my search. There were deposits being made on litters that were not even conceived yet.

Then finally, a kennel owner responded to my email. One of his German shorthair studs had sired a litter of six, two black-and-white females included. It was time to tell my husband I had found a puppy. But six hundred miles from our home.

In his often-analytical way, my husband said, "So what do you know about these puppies?"

"Not very much. I know it doesn't make sense, but I miss Kaiser so much," I said as tears rolled down my cheeks.

He put his arm around me. "Let's start by contacting the owner, see if the pups are still available. Maybe they can send pictures. Information about the dam. Something to help us know about these dogs before we consider an eleven-hour drive. Okay?" Home for us is remote, off the grid, on the Brule River in the woods of

Michigan's Upper Peninsula. A place we call BruleRidge. With winter firmly upon us, travel was a serious consideration.

The owner sent photos. What can you tell from six little roly-polies climbing over each other? Of course, they are cute. Aren't all puppies cute? Does cute make a companion for life? Show us the two females, the black-and-white ones. More photos came.

"That one is so cute, but she really looks like a Saddleback piglet," I said. "Look at that round little body with that big strip around her middle."

"How about the other one, the one with the round spots on her back?"

More pictures arrived. The little girl with three silver-dollar-sized black spots on her ticked body, sitting proudly on a hand-knit afghan, a Christmas tree in the background.

"We have to decide," I said. "I'm sure other people are interested. Black-and-white pups are so hard to find." I was fearful we would lose this opportunity.

"Let's enjoy Christmas, then we'll make up our minds, okay?"

Christmas Eve message to the breeder: "We will let you know our decision the day after Christmas. Have a wonderful holiday."

On Christmas morning I accessed my email, and a picture of the black-and-white German shorthair puppy with three spots on her back wearing a bright red holiday bow opened before me.

"Oh honey. Look at this!"

With all logic discarded, we made a decision, that very moment, fueled solely by emotion. We sent an email to the owner. "We want that puppy, the one with the big red bow. And a very merry Christmas to you."

With our check in the mail, she was almost ours. What would we call this little miss? German royalty? Nothing seemed to fit. How about European royalty? Not a queen. Possibly a countess? A list of names had developed that included Tessa, Mika, and Sasha. A second list of new puppy names arrived from our granddaughter. Sasha was on her list as well. With two votes, the new puppy was christened Countess Sasha of BruleRidge.

Just days after Christmas, we left the Upper Peninsula with a kennel and a change of clothes in the back of our SUV and drove the six hundred miles on snow-covered roads to meet the new denizen in our home. After a long day driving, we checked in to a hotel a few miles from the address we had been given. Like two nervous parents making a test run to be sure they would make the hospital in time for a delivery, we made a trial run from the hotel, driving by the owner's house to ensure we allowed enough time in the morning. We had to be there by 7:30 a.m. so the owner could get to work. We fitfully slept until daybreak. We sipped coffee at the hotel. Finally, time to go.

We parked in the driveway. I patted my husband's knee. "Here we go." I got out of the car. The glow from a distant streetlight dimly lit the doorway.

When I knocked on the door, chaos broke loose. A cacophony of barking dogs and yipping puppies and a voice loudly exclaiming, "Shut up!" I had to fight the flight instinct. What had we done? After the second rap on the door, a slightly disheveled woman wearing a bathrobe appeared. She apologized for the bedlam and pointed at another door, which led to the garage. "They're in here." I beckoned to my husband, who was getting out of the car.

Light in the garage was marginal. There seemed to be constant motion in a raised puppy pen situated in the middle of the floor. As I watched the blur of fur bodies, I realized there were two types of puppies—German shorthairs and something else. "You have two litters of puppies?" my husband asked.

"Yup, one planned and one not. You know, a fence jumper." No further explanation. "This one is yours." She scooped a puppy from the masses and thrust her into my arms. "I'll get the papers."

We could see the dam in the kitchen, a beautiful shorthair, obviously distressed at being separated from her puppies. The owner returned, handed us the papers, thanked us for the check, said what I thought was, "She hasn't eaten," and quickly dismissed us.

Even though we brought a small kennel, the thought of putting the puppy alone in the back of the car after snatching her from her siblings seemed too cruel. "I'll hold her for a little while, let her adjust to us." After just a few blocks driving, warm wet dog food soaked my sweater. I realized the woman must have said, "She just ate." We pulled into a gas station, where I made a quick change of clothes. Little Sasha slept on my lap the remainder of the eleven-hour trip to her new home.

The Christmas tree was still up when we returned home. With her instincts as a bird dog, Sasha followed her nose and soon found the excitement of ornaments and gifts. Of course, there were several puppy presents wrapped and ready—lots of chew toys, a new bed, a red-and-black tweed knit sweater, and even a small camouflage fleece blanket from friends. That became Sasha's security. She still drags it around and takes it to bed like a toddler.

At our first visit to the vet, we shared that Sasha seemed to have a very difficult time during late afternoon and the dinner hour, acting out, being naughty. The vet looked at us and said, "Don't you remember a too-tired toddler? That's what you have here." The next stop that day was the pet store. We left the store with an armload of ploys designed to distract and develop patience in our little toddler. The best was a Kong we filled with her food. It took most of our dinner hour for her to roll it until she got all of her kibble out of a small hole.

The contrast in her behavior came when she would crawl onto my husband's chest and fall asleep with her head in the crook of his neck. I was sure as I watched them that he was dreaming about a future grouse hunt. At the same time, as her feet twitched, I was hoping she was dreaming about a good life, running through the woods, a mile from the nearest road, on the bank of the beautiful Brule River.

In spite of the temperature being well below zero and the snow at least two feet deep in the Upper Peninsula, the Countess Sasha of BruleRidge had arrived, demanding center stage, and she has never stepped into the shadows. She is sweet and sassy. She is athletic and affectionate, inquisitive and intelligent. She is a wild child. She is Daddy's little girl. The Countess Sasha was, and is, one of our best-ever Christmas gifts.

26

Juggling Glass Ornaments

Nicole M. Miller

I was working full-time, mothering a one-year-old, pregnant with another on the way, and about to lose my mind.

In February that year, we'd had to say farewell to our seven-year-old dog, and it hit us hard. In June, I'd attempted to fill that particular dog-sized hole in my heart with a new puppy.

I was losing my mind.

Our firstborn son was six months old when we walked into the dog rescue and picked up a little golden fluff ball. I thought I'd be able to handle it all. She had the look of a lab, pit bull, and cattle dog all rolled into one, with deep eyes and furrowed forehead that gave her such a look of innocence.

Clearly, I'd forgotten what puppy life is like.

By Christmastime, I was ready to break.

The dog had peed over nearly every square inch of the house. We could never get her outside soon enough. She'd poop on the floor in front of me while I nursed our six-month-old son. During her kennel training, she would still soil her bedding and shred the rest. She shredded dozens of children's toys, no matter how we tried to barricade her away from them. She refused to sleep through the night, always picking an opposite schedule to whatever the six-month-old was sleeping or not sleeping that night. And any morning when the kid would let us sleep past sunrise, the puppy was sure to demand her own attention.

All I wanted for Christmas that year was my sanity. And my other dog back.

This wasn't me. This wasn't how I operated. I was capable, strong, and an animal-lover to my core. I'd grown up taking care of other dogs, horses, cats. I was responsible; I thrived under this sort of pressure.

Of course, that was before I had a child. Suddenly, I wasn't sure who this new version of me was.

Old me never would have broken down and cried when a puppy pooped on the floor next to our pile of wrapped presents. Old me never would have screamed at the dog when it whined. Old me never would have imagined contemplating taking the puppy back to a shelter.

I didn't give up like that.

That wasn't who I was.

And yet, it was all I wanted for Christmas.

The last year had been our first as parents and our last Christmas with the dog we could never replace.

This year, I wondered if it'd be the last with the new dog too. I was juggling a thousand glass balls over my head, like shiny ornaments all waiting to fall with the single misstep.

In a season when I typically look forward to breaking out the decorations tote and doing small garnishes here and there, when I love blasting Christmas music and dancing to it whimsically, I was distracted to a state of rage.

Each ornament glittered and winked at me, taunting me. Which would fall first? And would I just let them all fall?

I hated Christmas in those moments. I hated one more thing. I hated the reminder of the sweet Christmas season we'd shared the year before with the dog we'd loved so dearly.

The dog so opposite of this annoying puppy.

I was caught in a spiral of self-hate and frustration.

I couldn't hear God, no matter how much I prayed and begged for an answer. What was I supposed to do?

How could I juggle it all?

But somehow, the Christmas season dawned, and I saw clearly which ornaments to let fall from my grasp.

Perfectionism crashed. *Who needs perfect Christmas cards anyway?*

My need to please everyone crashed. *My family matters. My soul matters.*

The unrealistic expectations I held myself to crashed. *Life in chaos is okay, as long as everyone is safe, healthy, and loved.*

I came to terms with it all. Even the most well-behaved dog would have been a lot more for me to handle during that season. It wasn't her fault. She wasn't a bad dog. She was a normal puppy.

That Christmas was wild, joy-filled, and chock-full of photos of the six-month-old puppy, the one-year-old toddler, and my bulging pregnant belly.

Our one-year-old came into his own that season, stumbling around and chasing the puppy on his hands and knees. They instantly became bonded, and I saw what would become their lifelong friendship solidified in those Christmas days.

Life was full and rich and utterly messy.

I learned to let go, and I also learned to keep the real, non-metaphoric ornaments far away from the dynamic duo that was our son, Anthony, and the puppy, Dany.

Dany's presence and rocky introduction to our family served as a steep learning curve for me. I had to learn to adjust, and later I'd see how the lessons I'd learned in this messy phase of life prepared me in a small way for life with two toddlers (and a one-year-old dog).

Dany couldn't fill the void left behind from the dog we'd lost. But she carved an entirely new place within my soul. That Christmas wasn't her last with us as a family. Every year, we've grown closer, she and I. Our bonds are stronger with each passing day. She's a fierce protector of our children, and after some training, she's a fine farm dog. I jog with her, bring her along on all my chores, and turn to her often for snuggles.

There's still the occasional shredded diaper, torn-up toddler toy, and puddle on the floor, but I think she does it to remind me of the "old days." I'm not nostalgic for those, but it is a powerful reminder of all that we've overcome.

That glass ornament is firmly in my grasp, and it's now one that I'm not letting go.

27

A Puppy for Christmas

Catherine Ulrich Brakefield

A horse neighed in the adjoining stall. A whiff of saddle soap and leather and the clomping steps of a Dutch Warmblood echoed near me. *Where could they be?*

Then I heard it. A symphony of unmistakable little whines that captured my heart. Puppies! Could there be a better present beneath a sparkling Christmas tree than a fun-loving, frolicking puppy?

"Here you go," said the owner of the litter. He plucked a female from the litter of Jack Russell terriers and handed her to me.

My husband, Edward, looked at the remaining five puppies trotting after mom and her flapping milk supply, then looked back to the squirming bundle of fur in my arms. "Are you sure she's weaned?"

The owner glanced at the pups following their mother around the stall. "Can't blame them for tryin'." He chuckled. "My pups have been on puppy chow for over a week and doing well."

The pup in my arms was the largest of the Jack Russell litter. She looked up at me with those big brown eyes of hers, and my heart melted. Edward handed over the cash.

I named her Tippy, after my first dog, Tip. So what if Tip was a male and this little puppy was a female? I was confident she would live up to her namesake, the dog who brought me through some adventurous experiences during my preadolescent years. In the back of my mind, I hoped this little bundle of squirming fur would be the confidante to my children that my first dog was to me.

Now in our car, I had Tippy safely tucked in my arms. Her little puppy tongue licked my cheeks, and her sweet puppy breath perfumed my nostrils. However, she wasn't satisfied with demurely sitting in my lap. She squirmed, whined, and then let out a baby yip. "Did that noise come from you?" I promptly received a lick. "How are we going to keep her a secret until Christmas?"

My husband and I were on the same wavelength. "She might be harder than you think to hide in the same household with Kim and Derek," Edward said. "We still have a week before Christmas." He slowed the car down, the gravel of the road crunching beneath our tires. "Maybe we should turn around and see if the owner of the litter will allow us to keep her at the stables until Christmas Eve?"

I must have looked at him with something that resembled hysteria.

"It'll only be a week, Cathy." He rolled his eyes at me. "Come on, it's a puppy, not a baby."

I can't explain the feeling that washed over me. Maybe it was my maternal instinct coming to the surface. How could I relinquish something so needy and defenseless? I felt this puppy and I had bonded. After all, hadn't I allowed her to lick my face? That had to mean something. "We can do this, hon." I was happy that my voice sounded reassuring, because I hadn't a clue how we were going to make it happen.

As we drove into our driveway, an idea materialized. "Edward, she was born in a stable. Why don't you fix her a nice place in our last empty stall? I think there's a box in the garage that will work perfectly. We can make a bed of straw in there, and she just might be content."

Edward looked at me skeptically. "You mean where I keep Merlin?"

Merlin was our goose. Ever since he'd lost his mate, he'd not been too friendly to animals. Lately, he had taken it upon himself to guard the yard. He was the official watch goose of the premises. No, I didn't want to take a chance on him picking on our little puppy.

"What about the tack room?"

"I guess I could lock the door, but more than likely, Tippy will whine when she hears the kids doing their chores."

"Okay, before Kim and Derek get up, I'll move her to our bedroom."

Tippy whined. That just about broke my heart. I'd be leaving her alone on her first night away from her mom, sisters, and brothers. I cuddled her closer.

"Yeah. I can see that happening." Edward chuckled.

The first night with a new puppy is often a nonsleep experience. We kept Tippy in the stable until both children retired for the evening. Then Edward, with Tippy hidden inside a big purse, sneaked her into our bedroom and placed her in the box I had readied. Lucky for us, our bedroom was on the first floor and our children's rooms on the second floor.

Our new little girl let me know that she wasn't just any ordinary puppy. She didn't cry at night. Didn't whimper for her mommy, brothers, or sisters. Our eight-week-old puppy handled the transition into her new home admirably.

This little Jack Russell bundle of white, black, and brown patches proved more than capable of coping with the Christmas chaos. The tinsel and sparkling lights that made the snowflakes dance like hundreds of diamonds enticed Tippy to pounce, leap, and yip in joyous pleasure. Edward and I took turns enjoying the splendors of glistening snowflakes twinkling beneath a moonlit sky as we walked Tippy out at midnight, confident that our children were fast asleep.

Fortunately, Derek was in the first grade and Kim in the sixth grade that year, so their absence during the day made Tippy's first few days at our house fairly easy. By the time the kids' Christmas break rolled around, my handbag had become Tippy's second home. I would nestle her inside, place my index finger to my lips, and whisper, "Shush." She'd turn her tiny head from side to side, give a small whimper, then settle into silence. My husband and I could carry her without her whining.

"What's in there?" Derek asked one day when I needed to get Tippy out for a potty break.

I avoided the question. "Did you get your chores done? You and Kim can't go *anywhere* until they're finished."

My children had cousins who lived about a quarter of a mile away, and the cousins were constantly together. They were either over at our house or my children were at theirs, which made it especially nice on weekends, holidays, and summer breaks.

While the kids were away, Tippy ran and plunged into the one-foot snowdrifts, burying herself headfirst, but she didn't care. I think being born outside made her more comfortable outdoors and helped her to know where to do her business.

Some families open their gifts on Christmas Eve. But we like to keep that time for church and reflecting on the true meaning of Christmas. Edward and I were tempted to give our children an early gift. We figured after a week of vigilance, we could use a good night's sleep. We only had one more day to go, so we resisted the temptation.

That Christmas Eve, our pastor read from the book of Luke: "And this will be the sign to you: You will find a Babe wrapped in swaddling cloths, lying in a manger" (2:12).

I hugged Edward's arm and whispered, "Our puppy was born in a stable just like our Savior."

I knew from waiting for a foal to be born that a stable in the wee hours of midnight could be scary. Night critters like bats, mice, raccoons, and possums made all sorts of noises in the creepy blackness. I understood an animal entering the world in a stable, but it was hard to imagine a newborn baby wrapped in pieces of discarded swaddling cloths lying in a cold, drafty stable in a cow's feeding trough. The image of that hit closer to home on this Christmas Eve.

That night, I couldn't sleep. I felt like a child again, imagining the elation upon my children's faces. And I felt joy in my heart for that babe in the manger.

When I heard voices upstairs, I shook Edward awake. "Hurry, Kim and Derek are up," I whispered.

The moon still hung like a giant spotlight in the twinkling heaven. Edward stumbled out of bed, walked to the edge of the stairs, and listened. He turned. "Get Tippy in her box. I'll try and stall them." Quietly he crept upstairs. In his booming voice he said, "Why are you kids up so early?"

Murmurs followed.

I ran toward the Christmas tree, placed Tippy in the box, tied it up with a big red bow, and waited. Not a whimper. I smiled, remembering that first day Edward and I picked her up from the stables, the pup wiggly and whining for human affection.

Kim was first to the box. Derek was busy checking out his new bike.

"Is this present for both of us, Mom?" Kim said.

I nodded. "It's from Daddy and me."

Once Kim loosened the bow, the lid tipped upward, and out jumped Tippy like a jack-in-the-box. Her stubby white tail wagged a mile a minute as she yelped and barked.

Derek dropped his bike. "A puppy!"

Two pairs of hands stroked Tippy's smooth coat. Her little pink tongue licked my children's cheeks as they laughed.

Outdoors, the moon relinquished its throne for the coming sun, and the twinkling lights of our Christmas tree became less bright. We all walked outside with Tippy. Beams of light shot above the crest of the hillside as the sun peeked over the horizon.

"Look at that!" Edward shouted.

Sunlight touched the newly fallen snow. It twinkled back at us like thousands of sparkling diamonds, gleaming, easily within our grasp.

Thank you, God.

I was and still am grateful.

28

Forever Christmas

Marci Kladnik

It rarely snows in the hills above Santa Barbara, but when it does, crowds flock up there to play in it. We had a nice snowfall not long after Christmas the first winter my Scottish terrier, Maggie, was with me, so I took her up the mountain for the experience and because I wanted to see snow again myself.

We were lucky that, even though it was snowing lightly, the road wasn't closed. Forest rangers usually turn back cars without chains because coastal California drivers don't know how to drive in the snow. It wouldn't have mattered to the rangers that I'd spent eighteen adult years in Wisconsin and knew the slippery ropes of winter driving.

There were already lots of cars parked along the roadside near a good clearing, but I managed to find a spot where I wouldn't get stuck, and I pulled in. Maggie was watching a few dogs frolicking in the snow and people building snowmen or throwing snow-balls as she danced back and forth across the back seat, eagerly waiting for me to let her out. She was barely a year old and still channeling her inner puppy.

When I opened the door for her, she jumped down immediately but stopped, mystified. Maggie was tentative at first, stepping gingerly over the cold snowy grass until her Scottish heritage kicked into high gear, and she began to dash around like the puppy she still was. Once across the road and off leash, she began snowplowing and rolling in the snow and dashing up to people and dogs to say hello. I could just imagine her exclaiming to everyone, *Isn't this sooo cool?!?* She was in her element, running here and there to sniff and play. I could almost hear the giggles that were surely in her heart.

We walked a hundred yards away to an area void of people and other dogs. Maggie and I were alone now in a pretty little meadow bordered by low hills and a few scattered live oak and pine trees. It was our own magical place of peace, quiet, and serene beauty slowly being covered by the softly falling white flakes. The snow did fall softly, but the tiny sound each flake made as it struck the ground around us combined together to give a light, almost feathery rustle to the air, adding to my delight.

Maggie ran ahead, glancing back at me now and again to be sure I was following. Dry grasses and weeds along with a few too-early bright spring flowers poked up through the snow.

Half-buried sticks and stones made walking treacherous for me with my fused spine, so I picked my way carefully and slowly along the route Maggie had chosen, keeping her in sight all the time and trying not to slip, trip, or fall. There was no danger of her running into a street, and I wasn't worried she'd run off as she dashed hither and yon ahead of me.

The snow was on the slushy side with the temperature just barely freezing and the ground not frozen. It was great for those making snowmen and snowballs, but my shoes and pant legs were soon soaked. I always had the groomer give Maggie a "Scottie cut," so with her being low-slung and with her skirt of long hair,

I knew she would be a total mess when we got back to the car. No matter, my puppy was having the time of her life. As for me, I was at peace with the great beauty surrounding me and with the spirit of the Christmas season still in my heart.

The clouds were low and showering us with tiny flakes, but as we walked in the meadow they parted in the distance to a beautiful blue sky, and sun burst out on the hills before us. Maggie was far ahead of me, exploring everything and loving the snow. It was easy to keep her in sight, a moving black blob with a bright red harness on the field of white.

We stayed about an hour until my feet began to get too cold. Maggie could have played in the snow for another hour or more, but I called her to me. It was time to go home. Thankfully she came running back, and we headed to the car. One happy puppy, she was still grinning and prancing the whole way.

As expected, Maggie was a mess. Balls of dirty ice and snow clung to her skirt, and her feet were muddy. Her beautiful harness, no longer red, was soggy and mud-caked, but her eyes were bright with excitement, so what did it matter?

As dirty as Maggie was, I didn't want to put her in the back seat. I always carried an old pink blanket in my car, one I'd picked up years before at a garage sale for a dollar. It was one of my best purchases ever and had saved my car from all sorts of filth for many years. Now I spread the blanket out in the back of the little SUV and put Maggie on it for the ride back home and the warm baths that would follow for us both when we got there.

I took a lot of photos to document the outing that day, and they showed a very happy black Scottie puppy, beautiful in her harness bright red against the snow. This was before digital cameras were everywhere, so I had to wait for the prints to come. When they arrived, I shared them with my parents. My dad, being an artist, asked for the panorama shots I'd taken of Maggie sitting in the middle of the snowy meadow, facing the hills with the sun shining on them.

Although the photos have faded and my dear father and Maggie are both gone, I still have the wonderful painting Pop did of the scene to remind me of that happy day. It will always be my "Forever Christmas" painting that hangs in the home office above my desk.

29

Mithril's Bell

Claudia Wolfe St. Clair

Now that I'm taking Christmas decorations down and putting them away, I have time to reflect on the memories each ornament evokes.

My Christmas decorations are like a life review. Those of us who add an ornament every year know what I mean—the ones our children made, the ones we were given all take us back to a specific moment in time.

Christmas decorating is always a festive task. Boxes open and ornaments appear while the helping hands of children and grandchildren get involved. It's joyous pandemonium.

At the other end, when visits are over and New Year's has come and gone . . . well, a quieter experience presents.

For me it has become a time to slip into specific memories each ornament delivers like pages in a favorite book. Most bring a smile; some make me laugh out loud. Others bring a tear, but they all hold cherished memories.

The year our first child was born at Fort Bragg was also the year our dog Mithril joined the family. Those two are forever linked in a Christmas memory that still makes me laugh out loud.

Mithril, a terrier mix, was just a puppy, but growing at an alarming rate. She was particularly interested in what was going on in the kitchen. Who can resist the smell of bacon cooking? Not Mithril.

The hubris of a first-time mother preparing six quiches for a party, trying to do too many things at once . . . what a life lesson that was! The production line was set up on the counter with ingredients added one after another. Onions? Check. Mushrooms? Check. Bacon? Check. All the while Mithril keeping me company.

Custard filling was made and in the first two pie tins when the baby cried to be fed. Adjourning to the living room and a comfortable spot, I settled in to nurse the baby. That was always a sweet time and calm respite.

Then I heard it. A quiche pan hit the floor. *Oh no!*

To my horror I caught Mithril lapping up the custard from the second quiche. The first was a completely empty pan on the floor. Mithril! She was stretched up, paws on the counter, making the quiches disappear. I had no idea of the extent of her reach. She looked guilty but satisfied as she retreated from the kitchen. I assessed the damage while the baby screamed in protest of the interrupted feeding.

Well, one quiche gone. The custard in the second partially consumed. Did I toss it? Or did I pretend nothing happened?

Maybe I cooked and served it anyway. I am not telling.

That's why I still laugh when I hold the ornament from that Christmas.

Mithril had a way of taking advantage of my distractions. She was clever and quick. She was also a well-traveled girl.

Our next assignment took Mithril and the family to the Republic of Panama. Our quarters on Fort Davis were on top of a hill with a view of ships in the Panama Canal.

Preparing for Christmas on the isthmus was always a joyful time. The trade winds returned, and the rainy season stopped. The best part was knowing that my parents, brother, and grandfather would be joining us for the holidays. We spent three Christmases in Panama. Each year my family made the trip. Every year ornaments were added to mark a significant event like the birth of our second child.

Our last Christmas in Panama, we had to put the tree in a playpen to keep the baby out of it, and Mithril too. She had adjusted to the tropics, but that pine tree was a thing of interest.

Once again, we had a kitchen incident. The turkey dinner was just a pleasant memory. My family was out for a walk while I stayed back to make turkey soup. I put the turkey carcass on the counter. It was perfect with ample drippings in the pan. This was going to be a great soup.

The baby woke from her nap upstairs. I pushed the pan to the wall and left to feed and change her. With feeding and changing accomplished, she was clean and happy, so now I could get back to making soup. There sat the pan where I'd left it. Empty. No carcass, no drippings, nothing. It looked as if it had been washed. Mithril was nowhere to be seen.

I took the clean pan to the living room and looked for Mithril. She sheepishly came out from hiding. She had managed to eat all of it without making a sound or dropping the pan. By some miracle she was unaffected by her caper. Unbelievable. All these years later I still think of her every time I make turkey soup.

By the time we were assigned to Fort Myer, Virginia, a third child had come along. We'd bought a home outside the Beltway. That Christmas we had the biggest, most beautiful tree we'd ever had. The only place it fit was in the archway between the living and dining rooms. It filled the space side to side and was gorgeous from both rooms.

It also blocked Mithril's usual path to the back door.

Anyone who has a dog knows there are ritual pathways through a house. It also doesn't matter what physical object is introduced in that pathway. A dog's gotta do what a dog's gotta do. Mithril found a way under and through the tree to get to the back door. Ornaments fell, needles dropped. A little rearrangement of ornaments was required so nothing breakable was in her way.

One of those ornaments was a sleigh bell. I hung it where Mithril would bump it every time she passed through the tree. It became a reassuring jingle indicating where she was, heading for the door. That was my cue to come through the kitchen to let her out.

Today I am taking down my tree. The children are all married with families and pets of their own. Mithril herself is a beloved memory. I still hang the sleigh bell on the lowest branch of the tree as I have every year. It is always the last ornament I take down at the end of the season. I give Mithril's bell a little shake, smile a little, cry a little, as I tuck it into the ornament box.

It is a ritual I will repeat next Christmas. And the year after that for as long as I am able to put up a tree.

ABOUT *the* CONTRIBUTORS

Jeff Adams passed away during the editing of this book. He was an Arizona-based speaker and teacher and the author of *Encouraging Words: Rebuilding Your Dreams*. Jeff loved golden retrievers, movies, and best of all, Rosemary, his wife of thirty-eight years.

DeVonna R. Allison is a freelance writer/speaker and Marine Corps veteran. She and her husband enjoy live music events, traveling, and spending time with their grown children as well as their grandchildren. Her website is devonnarallisonauthor .wordpress.com.

Lisa Begin-Kruysman's writing on dogs has garnered multiple honors from the Dog Writers Association of America. Her platform, the venerable American tradition of National Dog Week, inspired her career as a dedicated dog-writer and advocate. She maintains a Facebook page dedicated to National Dog Week, where dog-lovers of all stripes unite and celebrate our four-legged companions fifty-two weeks a year! Originally from New Jersey, she now writes from the small coastal town of St. Marys, Georgia.

Catherine Ulrich Brakefield says, "My readers inspire my writing." She is the author of five faith-based historical romances: *Wilted Dandelions* and the four-book Destiny series, *Swept into Destiny, Destiny's Whirlwind, Destiny of Heart,* and *Waltz with Destiny.* She's written two pictorial history books and numerous short stories. See www.CatherineUlrichBrakefield.com for more information.

Mary C. Busha is the author of *Breaking the Power of Negative Words: How Positive Words Can Heal.* Now a full-time writer, speaker, and workshop and event coordinator, Mary spent most of her career working with other writers as editor, publisher, agent, and writer's coach. She is a wife, mother, and grandmother who enjoys reading, crocheting, and leading small groups at her church. She makes her home in Ocala, Florida, with her husband, Bob, and their rescue dog, Kaycee, and can be reached at mary cbusha@gmail.com.

Melody Carlson is one of the most prolific novelists of our time. With more than two hundred books published and sales topping seven million, Melody writes primarily for women and teens. She's won numerous honors and awards, including the RITA, Gold Medallion, Carol Award, and *Romantic Times* Lifetime Achievement Award, and can be found at melodycarlson .com.

Tracy Crump's book, *Health, Healing, and Wholeness: Devotions of Hope in the Midst of Illness,* released earlier this year. Her articles and devotions have appeared in a variety of publications such as *Focus on the Family, ParentLife, Mature Living, Upper Room,* and *Woman's World,* and she has contributed almost two dozen stories to Chicken Soup for the Soul books. Tracy co-directs Write Life Workshops, teaches at writers' conferences, is a freelance editor, and proofreads for *Farmers' Almanac*, but her most important job is grandma to the world's most adorable grandchildren. Visit Tracy at TracyCrump.com, SeriousWriter Academy.com, or WriteLifeWorkshops.com (where you can sign up for her newsletter plus story callouts).

Rhonda Dragomir is a pastor's wife and Bible teacher from Wilmore, Kentucky, with published works in Chicken Soup for the Soul anthologies and *Spark* magazine. She has won multiple awards, including being named 2019 Writer of the Year by Serious Writer, Inc. Rhonda is also a finalist in ACFW's 2020 Genesis Contest for her first novel, a sixteenth-century historical romance set in the Scottish/English borderlands. Read more about her on her website, www.rhondadragomir.com.

Chrissy Drew lives in Northern California with her darlin' Mike and their two-year-old pup, Tanner. She's been published in two previous Callie Smith Grant dog anthologies and eight other anthologies and is currently editing her first book in a contemporary romance series. She would love to hear from you. Find her at chrissydrew.com or facebook.com /AuthorChrissyDrew/.

Lonnie Hull DuPont is an award-winning poet, editor, and author of several nonfiction books. Her poetry can be read in dozens of periodicals and literary journals, and her work has been nominated for a Pushcart Prize. She is a member of Cat Writers' Association and Dog Writers Association of America, and her nonfiction is frequently about animals, including her memoir, *Kit Kat & Lucy: The Country Cats Who Changed a City Girl's World*. She lives in southern Michigan with her husband and two highly evolved cats.

Loretta Eidson writes romantic suspense. She is agented by Tamela Hancock Murray of the Steve Laube Agency and is a member of the Suspense Squad, ACFW, RWA, FH&L, SinC, and HACWN. Loretta lives in north Mississippi with her husband, Kenneth, a retired police captain. She loves salted caramel lava cake, dark chocolate, and caramel frappuccinos, and when she's not writing, she enjoys reading, cooking, and spending time with her family.

Denise Fleck was raised by a Great Dane and has spent her life loving animals. She has written scores of magazine articles, authored more than a dozen books, and is the proud recipient of both Muse Awards from the Cat Writers' Association and Maxwell Medallions from the Dog Writers Association, including "Best Children's Book." A former film studio publicist, Fleck followed her heart, leaving entertainment to work with animals, and developed her own Pet First-Aid & CPCR curriculum, personally teaching more than twenty thousand humans plus millions more via TV appearances. Learn more at www.PetSafetyCrusader.com.

Sherri Gallagher has been participating in K9 search and rescue since 1998, and her bestselling books (found on Amazon) are based on her own dogs or SAR team member canines. Her teen trilogy, Growing Up SAR, includes the novels *Turn, Go Find*, and *Bark Alert*. Her romance novels *Sophie's Search, Out of the Storm*, and *Pine Cone Motel* are all available as part of her series Searching the North Country. Her website is www.sherri gallagher.com, her Facebook page is SherriGallagherAuthor, and the team Facebook page is GSSARDA.

Lee Juslin is a freelance copywriter and author of the Nurse Frosty series of children's books. She also owns I B Dog Gone, a specialized embroidery business that is dedicated to supporting several terrier rescues as well as her TNR program, The Carolina

Cats. Visit her embroidery site at ibdoggone.com and on Facebook www.facebook.com/ibdoggone. Meet L'il B: www.hampshirehooligans.com.

Jenny Lynn Keller is a gal raised in the South who loves her Appalachian Mountain heritage and transforms her family's rowdy adventures into stories filled with hope, humor, love, and plenty of Southern charm. As a contributor to *Daily Guideposts* and frequent speaker about the history, culture, and beauty of the Great Smoky Mountains and surrounding area, she highlights Southern Appalachian folklore and places of interest through her weekly blog at www.JennyLynnKeller.com. Her true horse story, "A Pinto for Pennies," appears in Callie Smith Grant's *The Horse of My Dreams*.

Chris Kent retired from a career in marketing and public relations. She lives with her husband, two quarter horses, and Sasha, a German shorthair, in the remote Upper Peninsula of Michigan. She belongs to a group of north woods writers and is published in *Equus*, *UP Reader*, and *The Horse of My Dreams*. She enjoys gardening, making maple syrup, raising bees, horseback riding, fishing, volunteering in the community, and sharing these interests when grandchildren visit the north woods.

Marci Kladnik, her rescue dog, and three rescue cats have moved from sunny California back to snow country in central Wisconsin. A retired graphic designer and medical technical writer, she turned her talents to championing feral cats in 2007. She sat on the board of directors of Catalyst for Cats from 2007–2013 and wrote an award-winning cat column that ran in three newspapers and can be read on www.catalystforcats.org. Marci is an award-winning writer and photographer, contributor to www.catster.com and fearfreehappyhomes.com, and winner of the 2015 Kari Winters Rescue and Rehabilitation Award, and she served as president of the Cat Writers' Association from 2014–2018.

Andi Lehman freelances in diverse markets and writes nonfiction stories, articles, devotions, and grants. An author, editor, and popular speaker (live and virtual), she enjoys working with children and has just completed the first title in a series of conservation books for kids. Her education company, Life with Animals, teaches the wonder of all creatures and our responsibility to care for them. To learn more about Andi's work with words and animals, visit AndiLehman.com.

Marian McConnell lives in the beautiful Appalachian Mountains near Roanoke, Virginia, with her husband, Dano, and their dog, Lily. She's an artist, musician (three CDs), published author (*Emergence* and *Murder Hole: Catawba Murder Hole Cave*), caver, hiker, and motorcyclist. Marian McConnell is on Facebook, where you can see samples of her artwork, including the painting of Lily and Luca.

Nicole M. Miller is a People Operations Manager at Buffer, a writer, and a homesteader. She lives with her husband, two sons, and an assortment of dogs, horses, and chickens in southwest Washington and documents their adventures online at rusty acres.farm, on Twitter at @nmillerbooks, and on Instagram at @nicolemillerbooks.

Storytelling has been **Jane Owen's** passion since writing her first story, "Sparky's Gone," at age seven. She has enjoyed writing short stories, devotionals, and feature articles for *The Upper Room*, In Touch Ministries, Guidepost Books, St. Martin's Press, Bethany House Publishers, Worthy Media, Inc., and Standard Publishing, and "Christmas Vision" can be seen in Grace Publishing's *Christmas 2020 Moments* anthology. Jane and her husband, Ron, now live in Salt Lake City near their three wondrous grandchildren. Contact her at ladyjaneut@aol.com.

DJ Perry is the CEO of www.cdiproductions.com, an American motion picture company. Several of his screenplays have been produced into award-winning films, including The Quest Trilogy (*Forty Nights, Chasing the Star, The Christ Slayer*), *Wild Faith, Man's Best Friend,* and *Lost Heart,* just to name a few. Additionally, several of his screenplays have been novelized into books. DJ's stories in this book and in *The Horse of My Dreams* and *Second-Chance Cats* represent his next steps on his path of writing his own books. Visit his blog at www.djperryblog.com.

Amy Shojai is a nationally known pet care expert and a certified animal behavior consultant for cats and dogs. She is the award-winning author of more than thirty-five pet care books and a pet-centric thriller series featuring a German shepherd service dog. She lives in north Texas with Bravo-Dawg, Karma-Kat, Shadow-Pup, and the loving legacy of her furry muse, Fafnir. Visit her website at www.SHOJAI.com.

Kathrine Diedre Smith discovered her lifelong passion for animals at a very early age. While growing up in Texas, she lived in a remote, untamed area where nature and the wilderness nurtured her. She has worked extensively with zoological parks in reproductive physiology and conservation of endangered species, in addition to pursuing her strong passion and skills in animal behavior and strengthening the human-animal bond. Kathrine cares for and manages numerous kitties, feral cat colonies, and wildlife and is deeply committed to animal rescue, as well as inspiring positive changes.

Lauraine Snelling is the award-winning author of over one hundred novels, including the beloved Red River of the North series. When not writing, she can be found paintbrush in hand creating flowers and landscapes. She and her husband, Wayne, live in the Tehachapi Mountains in California with their basset, Annie, and one Buff Orpington hen, Millie, plus two brown Leghorn hens, Maggie and Mary, and a cat named Lapcat who does her best to keep them rodent free.

Claudia Wolfe St. Clair is an artist, writer, art therapist, and *anam cara* from Toledo, Ohio. She is the mother of three and grandmother of six. She and the love of her life are restoring the family home and gardens on Lake Erie. You can read more from Claudia in the Callie Smith Grant collections *The Horse of My Dreams*, *The Horse of My Heart*, *Second-Chance Dogs*, and *Second-Chance Cats*.

Connie Webster has been an animal lover since her earliest childhood. She lives in rural Michigan on the same farm where she grew up and raised her children. When she isn't riding trails with her friends or exploring the countryside with her grandkids, she adventures with her husband and tends her bees, horses, dogs, and one elusive cat.

Susan C. Willett is a writer, humorist, and blogger whose award-winning original stories, poems, and humor appear in print and online, including her website LifeWithDogsAndCats.com and on Facebook, Twitter (@WithDogsAndCats), and Instagram (@lifewithdogsandcats). You can read more of her work in Callie Smith Grant's books *Second-Chance Dogs* and *Second-Chance Cats* as well as in multiple Chicken Soup for the Soul books, including *The Magic of Cats* and *Listen to Your Dreams*. She shares her home with dogs Lilah, Jasper, and Halley as well as cats Dawn, Athena, Elsa Clair, and Calvin T. Katz, The Most Interesting Cat in the World™, whose photo went viral and now has his own social media accounts. Susan has plenty of inspiration for her work, often finding it hiding in a box, splashing through a mud puddle, or taking up an entire couch.

ABOUT *the* COMPILER

Callie Smith Grant enjoys animals of all kinds. She is the author of many published animal stories, the author of several biographies for young readers, and the compiler of the anthologies *Second-Chance Dogs* (awarded the Maxwell Medallion from Dog Writers Association of America), *Second-Chance Cats*, *The Horse of My Dreams*, *The Horse of My Heart*, *The Dog Next Door*, *The Cat in the Window*, *The Dog at My Feet*, and *The Cat in My Lap*.

ACKNOWLEDGMENTS

This is my ninth anthology of animal stories published by Revell, a division of Baker Publishing Group. This company is full of hardworking, dedicated people who have kept the ship sailing even during pandemic days. I thank you all for everything you do. Specifically, I continue to be grateful for my acquisition editor and friend, Dr. Vicki Crumpton, for believing and championing books like this one. She is brilliant and talented and fearless and a friend to all creatures. And I offer special thanks to President Dwight Baker for keeping Christmas books alive!

NOTES

1. "The Family Circus," MLive's *Jackson Citizen Patriot*, August 2, 2020.
2. "Good Week for . . . Getting That Puppy," *The Week*, August 7, 2020.

MORE Stories about the
Cats You Love

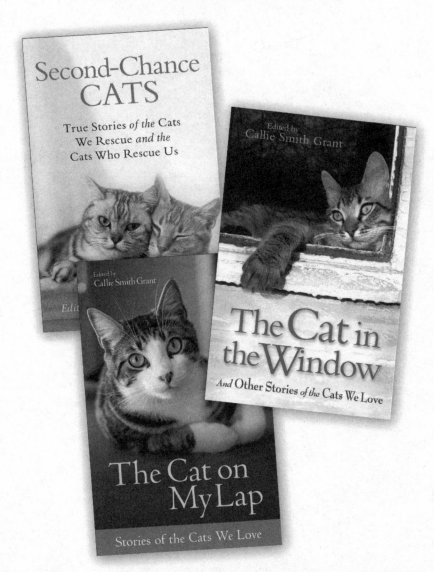

Revell
a division of Baker Publishing Group
www.RevellBooks.com

Available wherever books and ebooks are sold.

Paws to Read Some Stories about
THESE WAGGING FRIENDS

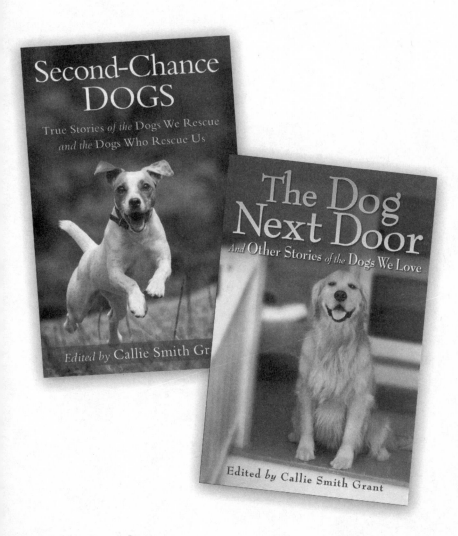

Collections of
Heartwarming Stories
for Horse Lovers

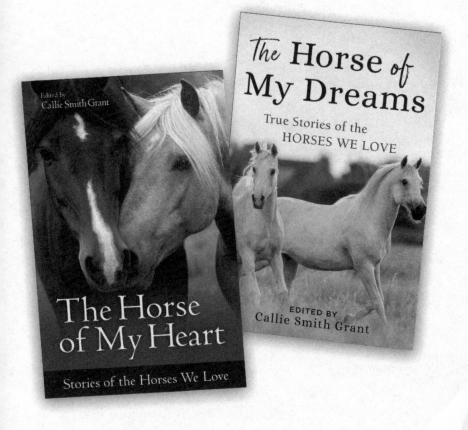

The Horse of My Dreams
True Stories of the HORSES WE LOVE
EDITED BY
Callie Smith Grant

Edited by
Callie Smith Grant
The Horse of My Heart
Stories of the Horses We Love

Revell
a division of Baker Publishing Group
www.RevellBooks.com

Available wherever books and ebooks are s